INSECTOSAURUS

Encyclopedia of Insects

General Editor   Tamara Green
Designer   Marilyn Franks
Cover Design   Lisa Robb
Principal illustrator   Neil Lloyd
Additional illustrators   Jim Channell
Tony Gibbons

Compilation copyright 2001 © Quartz Editions
Premier House 112 Station Road Edgware HA8 7BJ

First published in Great Britian in 2002 by Brimax, an imprint of
Octopus Publishing Group Ltd
2-4 Heron Quays, London E14 4JP
World English language license © Octopus Publishing Group

ISBN 1 8585 4433 5 (hardback)
ISBN 1 8585 4439 4 (paperback)
Printed in China

INSECTOSAURUS

Encyclopedia of Insects

BRIMAX

ABOUT THIS BOOK

There are two principal ways in which you can use this highly pictorial volume. Firstly, whenever you need to find out about a particular insect species or general aspect of insect life, consult the Index on page 190, which will take you direct to all relevant references. But you will also discover that, because of its clear, spread-by-spread format, the book is a delight to read from cover to cover. Featuring over 400 superb images accompanied by fully descriptive captions, this unique encyclopedia is packed full of information.

ACKNOWLEDGEMENTS

The creators and publishers of this volume wish to thank the following for supplying photographic images. Every effort has been made to include all contributors.

8tl SPL/C.Nuridsany & M.Perennou; tr BC/J.Cancalosi; 9 NHPA/M.Bowler; 10t BC/C.Fredriksson; 10b BC/K.Taylor; 11b SPL/D.Scharf; 12 OSF; 13 SPL/A.Syred; 14 SPL/K.Kent; 15c NHPA/G.I.Bernard; 15b NHPA/A.Bannister; 16bl SPL/M.Kage; 16br NHPA/N.A.Callow; 17cr SPL/J.C.Revy; 17br SPL/D.Scharf; 18 NHPA/S.Dalton; 19t SPL/A.Syred; b NHPA/K.Schafer; 20 BC/J.Burton; 21tl NHPA/M.Tweedie; tr BC/P.Zabransky; b SPL/C.Nuridsany & M.Perennou; 22t SPL; c OSF/N.Bromhall; b BC/K.Taylor; 23tl SPL/C.Nuridsany & M.Perennou; tr SPL/Dr.J.Burgess; cr SPL; br SPL/D.Scharf; 24cl SPL/C.Nuridsany & M.Perennou; bl SPL/A.Pasieka; 25tl SPL/A.Syred; tr SPL/J.C.Revy; bl,br C.Nuridsany & M.Perennou; 26 OSF/D.Scharf; 27t BC/F.Labhardt; c SPL/A.Syred; b NHPA/A.Bannister; 28 SPL/V.Fleming; 29t NHPA/A.Bannister; cl NHPA/G.I.Bernard; r NHPA/S.Dalton; br NHPA/E.Soder; 30t BC/P.Hinchcliffe; r NHPA/P.German; b OSF/T.Shepherd; 31 OSF; 32t SPL/A. & H-F.Michler; b BC/K.Taylor; 33t OSF/W.Cheng; b BC/G.Lockwood; 34 BC/A.Compost; 35cr NHPA/Dr.I.Polunin; bl OSF/D.Clyne; br NHPA/G.Bernard; 36tl NHPA/S.Dalton; cr SPL/C.Nuridsany & M. Perennou; bl BC/S.Prato; 37 BC/S.Prato; 38 BC/W.C.Ward; 39tl NHPA/S.Dalton; tr,r NHPA/N.Callow; 40tl BC/K.Taylor; bl SPL/C.Nuridsany & M.Perennou; 41tr BC/Dr.E.Pott; tl SPL; c BC/K.Taylor; b BC/A.Stillwell; 42tl OSF/K.Atkinson; tr OSF; bl OSF/P.Parks; br OSF/H.Taylor; 45 BC/Dr.F.Sauer; c SPL/Dr.J.Burgess; b NHPA/Y.Lanceau; 46 BC/J.Burton; 47t BC/M.Fogden; b OSF/T.Shepherd; 48 NHPA/A.Bannister; 49c OSF/S.Osolinski; r NHPA/P.German; 51t NHPA; b NHPA/M.Gardwood; 52t OSF/Animals, Animals; r BC/K.Taylor; b BC/J.Burton; 53 SPL/C.Nuridsany & M.Perennou; 54t SPL/G.Bernard; c BC/M.P.L.Fogden; b BC/K.Taylor; 55 SPL/W.Ervin; 56bl BC/K.Taylor; br SPL/G.Bernard; 57tl OSF/Animals, Animals; tr, br SPL/C.Nuridsany & M.Perennou; 58t SPL/A.H-F.Michler; bl SPL/V.Steger; 59t,c SPL/C.Nuridsany & M.Perennou; 60 SPL/S.Camazine; 61c OSF/D.H.Thompson; bl BC/K.Taylor; br NHPA/S.Dalton; 62tl SPL/Dr.J.Burgess; cl SPL/A. & H-F.Michler; tr SPL/Dr.J.Burgess; 63 OSF/R.Harvey; 64tl SPL/Dr.J.Burgess; tr SPL/C.Nuridsany & M. Perennou; cl SPL/W.Ervin; 65tl OSF/G.Carruthers; tr OSF/A.Root; 66 NHPA/S.Dalton;

67tl SPL/Dr.J.Burgess; r BC/J.Burton; 68bl NHPA/S.Krasemann; br SPL/C.Nuridsany & M.Perennou; 69l BC/L.C.Marigo; ct SPL/C.Nuridsany & M.Perennou; tr SPL/G.Dimijian; br OSF/Animals, Animals; 70 SPL/Dr.J.Burgess; 71 BC/J.Burton; 72 BC/G.S.Cubitt; 73t OSF/R.Blythe; c SPL/R.Coleman; b NHPA/S.Dalton; 74c SPL/Dr.M.Read; b NHPA/S.Dalton; 75 OSF/K.Sandved; 76 NHPA/S.Dalton; 77tl, br NHPA/S.Dalton; tr,bl BC/K.Taylor; 78 BC/Dr.J.Brackenbury; 79t OSF/K.B.Sandved; c OSF/A.Shay; b BC/K.Taylor; 80t NHPA/S.Dalton; b BC/K.Taylor; 81t NHPA/G.I.Bernard; b BC/A.Purcell; 82tl BC/Dr.F.Sauer; tr OSF/A.Shay; cl NHPA/S.Dalton; 83tr OSF/H.Fox; cr, br NHPA/S.Dalton; 84 NHPA/S.Dalton; 85tl SPL/K.H.Thomas; cr SPL/C.Nuridsany & M.Perennou; 86 SPL/Dr.M.Read; 87tr OSF/S.Camazine; br BC/K.Taylor; 89tl SPL/C.Nuridsany & M.Perennou; tr OSF/Animals, Animals; cr SPL; b BC/M.P.L.Fogden; 90t NHPA; b NHPA/O.Rogge; 91 NHPA/S.Dalton; 93t SPL/J.Shemilt; bl NHPA/N.A.Callow; br NHPA/G.Bernard; 94 BC/K.Taylor; 95tl OSF/C.Milkins; tr BC/K.Taylor; b SPL/C.Nuridsany & M.Perennou; 96t SPL; c SPL/J.C.Revy; b BC/K.Taylor; 97 SPL/E.R.Degginger; 98t SPL; b K.Grivas/Quartz; 99t SPL; c SPL/C.Wadforth; b SPL; 100t SPL/K.H.Kjeldsen; 101tl SPL/K.H.Kjeldsen; tr BC/K.Taylor; bl NHPA/Y.Lanceau; br SPL/M.Schaller; 102 t,c OSF/Animals, Animals; 103tl OSF/K.Atkinson; tr OSF/P.&W.Wood; cr BC/P.Kaya; 104 NHPA/A.Bannister; 105t NHPA/G.J.Cambridge; c BC/G.S.Cubitt; b NHPA/S.Dalton; 106t SPL/E.R.Degginger; c,b OSF/M.Fogden; 107t BC/K.Taylor; cl BC/S.Kaufman; 108t BC/J.Foot; c BC/E.Bjurstrom; 110tl BC/K.Taylor; tr BC/Dr.E.Pott; 111tl BC/K.Taylor; tr SPL/J.C.Revy; 112 NHPA/A.Rouse; 113tl OSF; cr BC/J.Foot; br OSF/B.Osborne; 114t NHPA/N.Bromhall; c NHPA/A.Bannister; b SPL/C.Nuridsany & M.Perennou; 115 SPL/C.Nuridsany & M.Perennou; 116 NHPA/A.Bannister; 117t BC/G.Cubitt; bl SPL/W.Ervin; br OSF/Dr.J.Cooke; 120t BC/K.Taylor; b NHPA/A.Bannister; 121t NHPA/S.Dalton; c OSF/S.Camazine; b NHPA/C.Ratier; 122bl BC/K.Taylor; br BC; 123tr BC/Dr.E.Pott; br SPL/C.Nuridsany & M.Perennou; 125 NHPA/J.Shaw; 126 BC/K.Taylor; 127tl BC/A.Purcell; tr SPL/Dr.J.Burgess; cr BC/K.Taylor; b BC/P.Kaya; 128t NHPA/A.Bannister; cl OSF/S.Camazine;

b NHPA/D.Heuclin; 129 BC/K.Taylor; 130t Nature & Science; bl,br,131bl,br SPL/C.Nuridsany & M.Perennou; 135tl,tr,cl,cr OSF/J.S. & E.J.Woolmer; 136 BC/K.Taylor; 137bl OSF/K.Atkinson; br NHPA/G.I.Bernard; 139l NHPA/J.Buckingham; r SPL/J.Burgess; 140t BC/K.Taylor; r OSF/J.Frazier; b OSF/H. Fox; 141 SPL/P.Menzel; 142t,c SPL/C.Nuridsany & M.Perennou; b OSF/G.I.Bernard; 143 tl NHPA/M.Tweedie; tr OSF/ G.I.Bernard; br BC/J.Brackenbury; 144t BC/J.Foot; bl NHPA/S.Dalton; 145 BC/J.Foot; 146tl NHPA/G.I.Bernard; c NHPA/S.Dalton; bl BC/C.Hicks; 148-9 SPL/P.Menzel; 150t OSF/ D.Thompson; cl BC/J.Burton; b NHPA/S.Dalton; 151 SPL/V.Steger; 152t OSF/D.Shale; c SPL/C.Nuridsany & M.Perennou; b SPL/V.Fleming; 154 OSF/D.Clyne; 155cr OSF/G.D.Plage; br NHPA/S.Dalton; 156tl OSF/J.Paling; tr SPL/Dr.T.Brain; bl OSF/M.Birkhead; 157 OSF/S.Camazine; 158 BC/K.Taylor; 159t OSF/A.MacEwen; c OSF/A.Ramage; b OSF/G.I.Bernard; 160 SPL/D.Schard; 161 NHPA/S.Dalton; 162 OSF/Dr.T.Brain; 163 SPL; 164t SPL/A.Syred; b OSF/C.Milkins; 165 OSF/D.Scharf; 166 NHPA/G.Bernard; 167t SPL/Dr.J.Brackenbury; bl OSF/G.Bernard; br BC/A.Purcell; 168 BC/K.Taylor; 169t BC/K.Taylor; b SPL; 171t SPL/S.Stammers; cl NHPA/J.L.LeMoigne; cr NHPA/N.A.Callon; 172t NHPA/S.Dalton; b NHPA/A.P.Barnes; 173t NHPA/A.Bannister; b SPL/J.Burgess; 175 NHPA/D.Heuclin; 176 BC/K.Taylor; 177c BC/ C.B. & D.W.Firth; b BC/F.Labhardt; 178 SPL/D.Scharf; 179tl OSF/M.Birkhead; tr SPL/S.Stammers; b SPL/M.Dohrn; 180t OSF/B.Kent; b OSF/R.Davies; 181cl OSF/M.Fogden; bl BC/P.Zabransky; 182tl OSF/K.Atkinson; 183tl OSF/C.Milkins; tr BC/Dr.F.Sauer; 184t BC/A.Purcell; 185c OSF/M.Cordano; b NHPA/M.Garwood; 186t NHPA/Dr.I.Polunin; c NHPA/D.Heuclin; b NHPA/E.Soder; 187t NHPA/A.Bannister

Abbreviations:
Bruce Coleman (BC); Natural History Photographic Agency (NHPA); Oxford Scientific Films (OSF); Science Photo Library (SPL); bottom (b); center (c); left (l); right (r); top (t).

CONTENTS

INTRODUCTION

Most insects are small in size, and a number are even tinier than the full point at the end of this sentence. With the naked human eye, therefore, you cannot see much, if anything, of their body structure, and it is often difficult to observe their behavior patterns. With the aid of a camera and sometimes a magnifying glass or microscope, too, however, you can zoom in. What wonderful surprises lie in store if you do so! In fact, why not amaze your friends by becoming an entomologist – or expert on insect life – in your own right! This book is designed to be your first guide to the science of entomology.

Throughout this fact-packed volume, alongside the fascinating text, there are hundreds of magnificent photographs and illustrations that, through magnification, provide unique insight into this curious miniature world. Some of its inhabitants are cute, as you will discover; but others are bizarre, and a few are known to be deadly.

Each of the eight sections in this book, has a differently colored border. The first section, called BODYWORK, is bordered in dark green. Turn to these pages for information about the structure of insects. Did you know, for instance, that they have no internal skeleton? Some are also amazingly strong, and others light up at times as they try to attract a mate.

Next comes a part all about insect HOMES. These pages have a light green border and present some of the most extraordinary dwelling places that insects make or choose. Some build intricate paper nests; others construct virtual skyscrapers; a few live within wood; and some can be found in structures called galls, while a number of species simply lodge in *our* dwellings.

In the chapter called LIFESTYLES, which has an orange colored border, we look at how insects hunt, hibernate, swarm, feed, prowl about by night, and defend themselves from their enemies.

Turn to the pink-bordered section, called ON THE MOVE, for information on the way insects get about. Some skim along the water; others excel at hopping; some species perform special dances; and others hover in the air. A few, meanwhile, hardly move at all for the whole of their lives.

Then discover which insects live in deserts, jungles, grasslands and cities in the bright blue-bordered section entitled HABITATS. And learn how insects reproduce and grow as you study the pages of the red-bordered chapter called LIFECYCLES.

In AROUND PEOPLE, a section bordered in yellow, you'll meet some of our insect enemies, such as those that sting or ruin our crops. as well as those most helpful to humans, such as aphid-eating ladybugs. Finally, in the dark blue-bordered pages of the section called RECORD-BREAKERS, you'll come face to face with the fastest, biggest, strongest, smelliest, and other insect champions.

We promise you much to marvel at as you investigate the wonderful world of mini-beasts!

BODYWORK

Do you always recognize an insect when you see one? A spider, for instance, is not an insect; nor is a centipede, nor a scorpion. For a creature to be classed as an insect in the strict sense of the word, it has to have certain physical characteristics. It will usually have three pairs of jointed legs when mature, an outer skeleton, and a pair of antennae on its head; three distinct body parts – a head, a thorax, and an abdomen; and sometimes, but not always, either one or two pairs of wings. Most insects are very small. The main reason for their small size is their lack of special breathing organs, or lungs, like ours. But being small has its advantages. Insects do not usually need large quantities of food and can creep into tiny crevices to hide from predators or to keep warm.

Join our team of entomologists (experts on insects) now as they take you on a guided tour of the bodies of a whole range of these fascinating creatures.

How do they see? How do they make sounds? How do they digest their food intake? How do they breathe? When did they first evolve? You are about to find out.

Prehistoric insects
Insects have existed since prehistoric times. Hundreds of millions of years ago, some – like this fossilized dragonfly – were far bigger.

On the wing
Some insects – dragonflies, for example – have very delicate wings. Others have wings that are protected by cases. Turn to pages 24-25 to discover what insect wings are made from and how different they can be.

Male and female
How do male insects differ from the females of their species? Are the males always larger? And how do they reproduce? Take a look at differences in male and female moths, bedbugs, stick insects and beetles on pages 18-19.

Listening legs
Is it possible for insects to hear if they have no ears? In some instances, they use two slits in their forelegs, which is what the katydid, shown opposite, is doing as she listens for a singing male. Other insects, such as moths, use special hearing organs in their thorax to pick up sounds.

NAMING

From the order Hymenoptera

The honeybee shown in the photograph above belongs to the species *Apis mellifera* and is now found all over the world, but is thought to have come from Asia originally.

An amateur entomologist has joined a field expedition that is looking for specimens in the wild and is lucky enough to come across an insect that he suspects is one of the largest known of its order. He makes some notes and takes a few photographs. Later, he will be able to confirm its identification. He knows that it belongs to the order *Coleoptera* because it is so beetlelike. But could it possibly be the rare *Goliathus goliathus*? This is the scientific name for the Goliath beetle.

Housefly

The housefly seen above cleaning its abdomen with its hind legs belongs to the order Diptera and the species *Musca domestica*.

True to its name

The Goliath beetle shown in the illustration above is named after the biblical giant who was slain by King David as a boy. It may grow up to six inches in length and is one of the largest of its order, the Coleoptera.

INSECTS

Insect orders

Ants/Bees/Wasps	*Hymenoptera*
Beetles	*Coleoptera*
Butterflies/Moths	*Lepidoptera*
Cockroaches	*Blattodea*
Dragonflies	*Odonata*
Earwigs	*Dermaptera*
Flies	*Diptera*
Grasshoppers	*Orthoptera*
Stick insects	*Phasmatodea*
Termites	*Isoptera*

We usually call insects by familiar names – butterflies, wasps, dragonflies, or bees, for example. But insects also have scientific names that help entomologists identify different species. In fact, a whole system of classification is used to refer to orders, families, genera, and other subdivisions.

Each type of insect within broader groupings also has a two-part Latin name. Take the Colorado beetle, for example. It belongs to the order *Coleoptera*, to the family *Chrysomelidae*, and has the Latin name *Leptinotarsa decemlineata*.

As you meet the insects presented in this book, you will find that we have always used their common names. It is sometimes helpful, however, to be able to recognize the experts' terminology.

Consult the table *above* if you would like to get to know the names of some of the main insect orders.

The number of species in some orders is very high. There are, for instance, 400,000 species of beetles and 150,000 species of butterflies and moths.

From the order Blattodea
The American cockroach of the species *Periplaneta americana* originally came from the state of Florida but is now a widespread pest in many countries.

Hindwing

Forewing

Abdomen

Leg

▲ Like a flower
Some insects, such as this flower mantis photographed in Borneo, look just like plants and are so well camouflaged by them that it is sometimes very difficult even for humans to distinguish them from blooms.

Gazing around at the world through the several thousand lenses of her compound eyes, a hornet wasp is preparing to go on the hunt. Her external skin, known as the *exoskeleton,* is very tough but lightweight and will protect her in any struggle to overcome a victim. Her bright coloring, fast movement, and stinger will stop even the most confident predators.

Although there are as many as 1.25 million known species of insects – and probably very many more that are still waiting to be discovered – there are nevertheless lots of features that they all have in common. Their bodies, for example, have three main sections. They are the head, the *thorax,* and the *abdomen.*

On the head of the majority of insects you will find their two *antennae* (or feelers), their eyes, and also their mouthparts.

Most insects have two compound eyes, while some have extra eyes, too. A few species, however, have no eyes, or just a small group of simple eyes.

The second section, or thorax, carries three pairs of jointed legs and, in flying insects, one or two pairs of wings. Sometimes, though, the first pair of wings is used as covers for the second pair.

OUTSIDE

A suit of armor
The hornet wasp below has a very tough exoskeleton that acts like a historical soldier's suit of armor, protecting the very soft inner organs if it is ever attacked by an enemy. Hornets are large members of the wasp family. The females sting less frequently than smaller wasps, however, and only if they are threatened.

The housefly, however, has converted its second pair of wings into stabilizers for use during flight. The abdomen, which is the final section, contains much of the digestive, circulatory, and respiratory systems, as well as an insect's sexual organs. Some also have a pair of appendages, known as *cerci*, at the tip of the abdomen. They play a role in sensing things.

A CLASS OF ARTHROPODS

Insects belong to a group of animals known as *arthropods*. Spiders are arthropods, too, but are not classed as insects because they have eight legs. In spiders the head, thorax, and abdomen are not in three sections as in an insect. Instead, the head and thorax are fused together.

One of the factors that has allowed insects to become so successful is their exoskeleton or *cuticle*. It is flexible and waterproof, with a waxy coating that stops insects from drying out in the heat. Despite its strength, the cuticle is very thin, its rigid structure provided by a substance that is called *chitin*.

Antenna

Eye

Thorax

Wonderful wing cases
The delicate flying wings of this black-spotted ladybug are protected by its elytra which are lifted for flight, as you can see in the photograph shown here. Ladybugs can squirt distasteful fluids if disturbed, and their bright coloring acts as a warning to predators not to approach them.

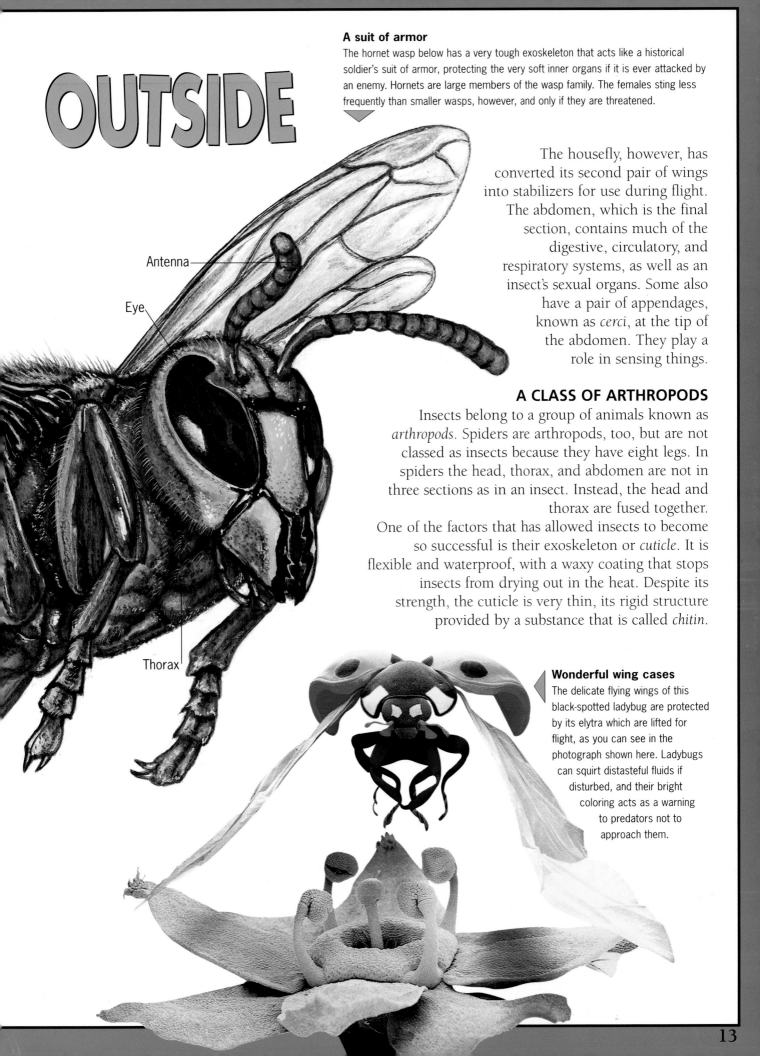

13

ALL LIT UP

It is early evening and getting dark. There are no street lights nearby, but suddenly, an eerie yellow light catches your eye, and within minutes you are startled as the whole area becomes bathed in a twinkling glow. During summer nights male firefly beetles take to the air. Once they are high enough to be seen from the ground, they start to signal in a form of sexual display and flash a bright yellow light from the tip of the abdomen. The females, who remain on the ground, will then flash a response. The males can now home in on potential mates. Each species of firefly beetle has its own code, so males will not usually be attracted to the wrong type of female.

Antenna

Abdomen

Bioluminescence

Flashing lights
Fireflies, visible as streaks of light in their mating season, have gathered over a farmyard in Iowa in this photograph. They are sending clear mating signals to announce one another's presence.

Chemical reactions

Most insects produce their bioluminescence in the same way. In that part of the abdomen where fat is stored, special organs have developed that contain light cells known as photocytes. They produce two chemicals, luciferase and luciferin. When mixed with oxygen from the the air and energy from the fat, they generate bioluminescence. The rate at which they flash is altered by changing the amount of energy produced by the tiny powerhouses, or mitochondria, that put out energy for the cell.

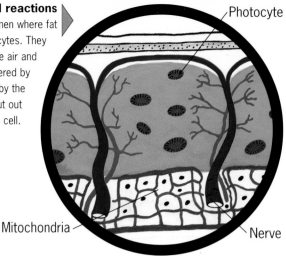

Photocyte

Mitochondria

Nerve

Twinkle, twinkle

Fireflies, like the one in this illustration, are often seen on summer nights as they twinkle a yellow or greenish light from their abdomens to attract a mate. The males flash in the air, and the females flash from the ground. They were even once kept in tiny cages to light up tropical homes.

Switching on

The click beetle right, photographed in Venezuela, has luminous areas on its head that show up like two sparkling eyes in the dark. Their larvae and even their eggs can be bioluminescent, too.

A lone firefly beetle is impressive, but sometimes tens of thousands of them can appear together. Whole fields can be lit up and will be visible up to a mile away.

Some insects, however, use bioluminescence to save their lives, and the color of light emitted varies from species to species. The male South American cucujo click beetle, for instance, can flash bright red and green when disturbed. The light produced is so unexpected and intense that predators back away, giving the beetle time to burrow into the soil to safety, or to fly into the air like a multicolored rocket.

Another use for bioluminescence is trapping prey. In certain caves in New Zealand, the ceilings sparkle with white lights created by the maggot of the fungus gnat. They attract flies and moths toward sticky threads of mucus in which they become trapped. The maggots can then feed on them at leisure.

On display

What a wonderful way to attract a mate! A female glowworm climbs up a stem to make herself more obvious and simply displays the luminous end of her body. Any male in the area will immediately be attracted to her. Both sexes can light up in this way, but the females excel at it.

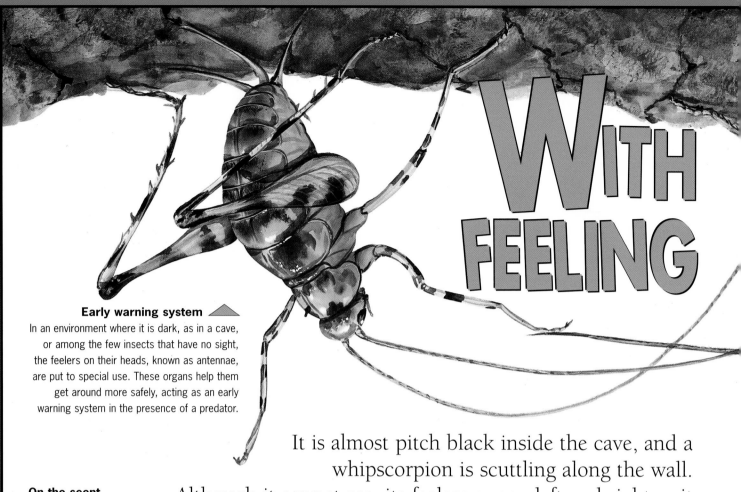

WITH FEELING

Early warning system
In an environment where it is dark, as in a cave, or among the few insects that have no sight, the feelers on their heads, known as antennae, are put to special use. These organs help them get around more safely, acting as an early warning system in the presence of a predator.

On the scent
The males of the black arches moth below have more thickly feathered antennae than the females. The males use them to detect the females' sexual attractants.

It is almost pitch black inside the cave, and a whipscorpion is scuttling along the wall. Although it cannot see, its feelers sweep left and right as it tries to find an unsuspecting victim, much as a blind person will use a white stick to find the way. Small insects have already fallen foul of this greedy predator; but fortunately for a nearby cave cricket with two extremely long antennae, there is a chance of escape. Before the whipscorpion gets close enough to strike, the cricket senses its approach and leaps to safety.

A tactile approach
This red ant has been photographed using its antennae as touch sensors to check out how stable a leaf surface is before crawling further along it.

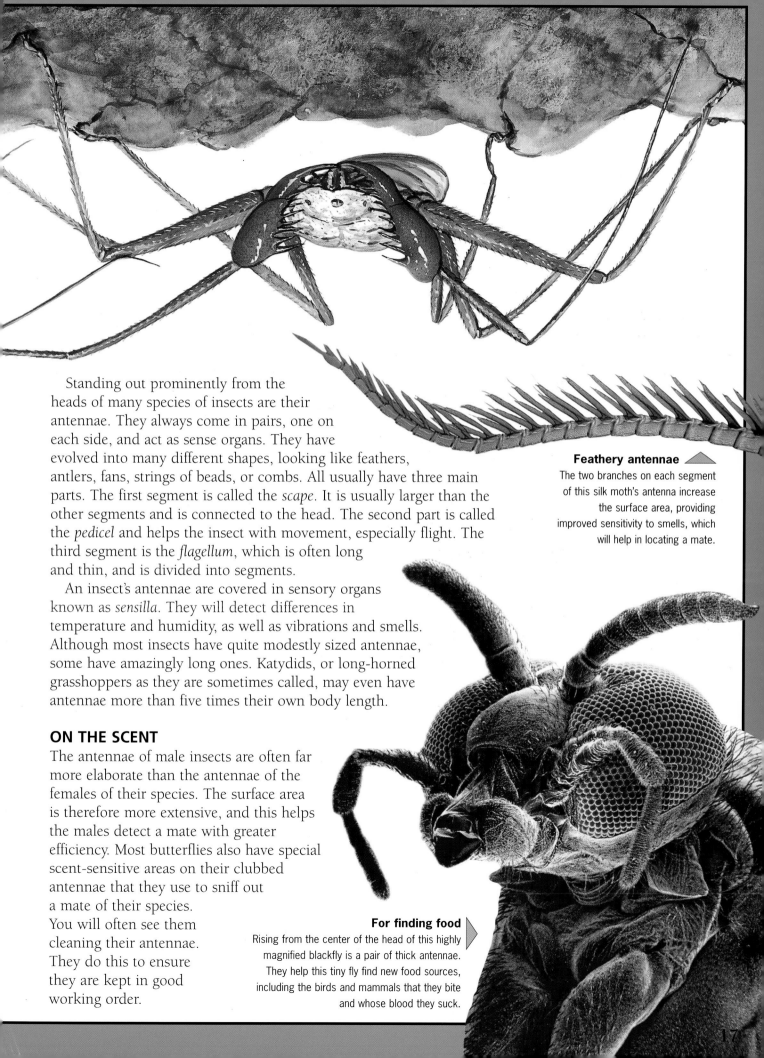

Standing out prominently from the heads of many species of insects are their antennae. They always come in pairs, one on each side, and act as sense organs. They have evolved into many different shapes, looking like feathers, antlers, fans, strings of beads, or combs. All usually have three main parts. The first segment is called the *scape*. It is usually larger than the other segments and is connected to the head. The second part is called the *pedicel* and helps the insect with movement, especially flight. The third segment is the *flagellum*, which is often long and thin, and is divided into segments.

An insect's antennae are covered in sensory organs known as *sensilla*. They will detect differences in temperature and humidity, as well as vibrations and smells. Although most insects have quite modestly sized antennae, some have amazingly long ones. Katydids, or long-horned grasshoppers as they are sometimes called, may even have antennae more than five times their own body length.

ON THE SCENT

The antennae of male insects are often far more elaborate than the antennae of the females of their species. The surface area is therefore more extensive, and this helps the males detect a mate with greater efficiency. Most butterflies also have special scent-sensitive areas on their clubbed antennae that they use to sniff out a mate of their species. You will often see them cleaning their antennae. They do this to ensure they are kept in good working order.

Feathery antennae
The two branches on each segment of this silk moth's antenna increase the surface area, providing improved sensitivity to smells, which will help in locating a mate.

For finding food
Rising from the center of the head of this highly magnified blackfly is a pair of thick antennae. They help this tiny fly find new food sources, including the birds and mammals that they bite and whose blood they suck.

17

MALE AND FEMALE

Male

Female

Swept off her feet
Just as Tarzan is often shown in movies picking up Jane, the male atlas beetle, after fighting off a rival, will lift up the female to proclaim himself the victor and carry her to a good spot so that they can mate. In the illustration below, you can see that the males and females of this species of beetle have great differences in their jaws.

He and she
Similar but not identical: the emperor moth on the left is a male, and on the right is the female.

On an oil-palm plantation in Southeast Asia a large atlas beetle has just finished fighting with a rival male. It was a closely fought match. The two of them had both been attracted by a female's seductive scent, and both were determined to mate with her. However, only one would win her favors. The two beetles therefore put their long horns to use and began to spar in the attempt to knock one another from a log, just as these insects always do when combat of this kind is underway. Eventually, one got the better of the other, and the victor claimed his prize, picking up the smaller female and carrying her off.

18

Like all living organisms, insects need to reproduce if their species is to survive. Their reproductive organs are in the abdomen and have their openings at the very tip. A male insect usually has a penis for transferring sperm from his body to that of the female. However, sometimes the sperm are transferred in a sac or *spermatophore*, which is either deposited on the floor and then picked up by the female, who instinctively places it in her reproductive system, or it is passed directly to her opening when the two of them get together.

IN SAFE STORAGE

In general, a single sperm will fertilize a single egg from the female. However, in many species the female is able to store sperm in special organs known as a *spermatheca*. Secretions produced in these organs can keep the sperm in good condition for long periods of time. Some queen ants can even store sperm for more than 15 years, releasing a quantity at intervals to fertilize their eggs. Not all insects reproduce sexually, however. Some are *parthenogenetic* and do not need a male's sperm to produce young. The grubs eventually emerge from eggs that have not been fertilized, and these offspring are usually all female.

Bed mates

Mating in bedbugs is unique among the insects. The male does not introduce his sperm into the female's opening as other insects do. Instead, he mounts her, punctures one of her abdominal segments, and deposits his sperm there in a little bag or sac.

Little and large

Some female stick insects are much larger than and very different from the males of this species, as you can see in this photograph of two of them mating. It was taken in jungle by the banks of the Napo River in the Amazon Basin, Brazil.

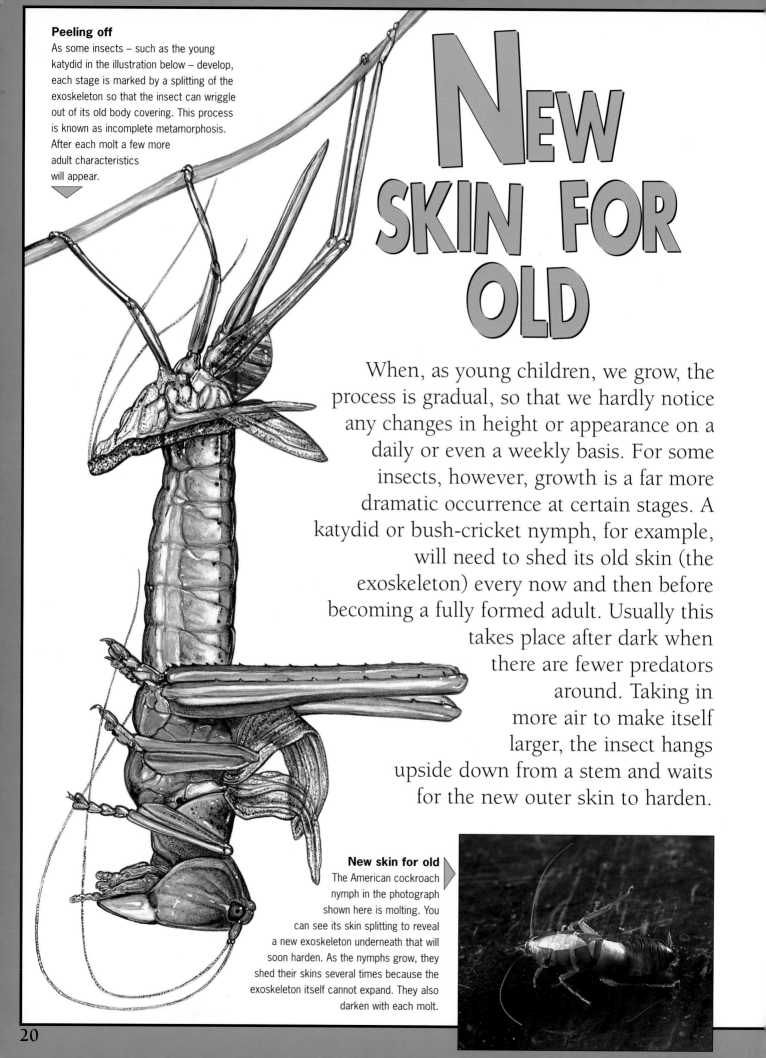

NEW SKIN FOR OLD

When, as young children, we grow, the process is gradual, so that we hardly notice any changes in height or appearance on a daily or even a weekly basis. For some insects, however, growth is a far more dramatic occurrence at certain stages. A katydid or bush-cricket nymph, for example, will need to shed its old skin (the exoskeleton) every now and then before becoming a fully formed adult. Usually this takes place after dark when there are fewer predators around. Taking in more air to make itself larger, the insect hangs upside down from a stem and waits for the new outer skin to harden.

New skin for old

The American cockroach nymph in the photograph shown here is molting. You can see its skin splitting to reveal a new exoskeleton underneath that will soon harden. As the nymphs grow, they shed their skins several times because the exoskeleton itself cannot expand. They also darken with each molt.

Castoffs ▲

On the banks of Europe's River Danube the photographer came across this old larval slough or discarded skin-covering of a dragonfly. It was shed as part of its final molt.

Skinned alive

There is no longer any life form inside the discarded skin of any insect that molts. This, for example, is the discarded skin of a desert locust.

▼

Breaking through

The short-legged wingless water springtails shown above shed their skins several times as they develop to maturity. You can see a few discarded pieces of exoskeleton floating on the water in this photograph.

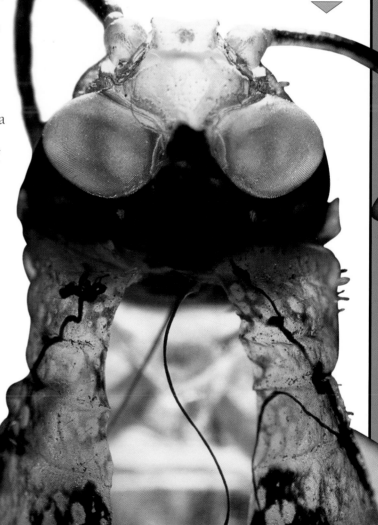

The external skeleton of an insect cannot increase in size and so must be shed when the larva has grown too large to be contained by it. This process is in some ways like a child growing out of his or her clothes and having to be bought new ones. The process is called *molting,* and it occurs at various times before maturity.

The first stage of molting usually involves the old cuticle separating from the *epidermis,* or layer of cells directly underneath it. While this is going on, the insect tends to stop eating and becomes lethargic. The epidermis, meanwhile, secretes a new soft and flexible cuticle. Increasing the amount of hemolymph in its body and drinking more water, the insect will now start to force its way out of the old cuticle. Once it has split, the new cuticle will gradually harden, forming a new exoskeleton for the larva. Until this stage is complete, the insect is vulnerable, since a short period of inactivity is involved. Strangely, however, some insects – the carpet beetle, for example – do not get larger after each molt but *decrease* in size.

JAWS!

With a flash of green, the spiked front legs of the praying mantis, shown in the central illustration, impale an unsuspecting butterfly. The mantis's jaws now slide easily through its victim's thin external skeleton. At the same time, the mantis's more sensitive mouthparts taste its meal.

Each insect species has evolved mouthparts to do specific jobs. The praying mantis's mouthparts are quite simple, and its jaws, or *mandibles*, act the same way as our own incisor (front) teeth. They have one sharp edge for cutting through food so that it can be swallowed more easily. On either side of the mandibles are two antennalike organs called *palps*. They are very sensitive and help the mantis to distinguish between substances that are safe to eat and others that may be poisonous to them.

Lip service

Insects do not use their mouthparts just for feeding. They can be put to many other uses. As with us, keeping clean is important for insects, too. Because their mouthparts are very sensitive, insects like the cockroach above can clean even the most delicate parts of their bodies – their legs and antennae, for instance.

Kiss and tell

Another use for mouthparts is communication. Insects, especially those that live in colonies, need to tell each other what is going on. In honeybees, for instance, the queen controls her hive by producing complex chemicals that tell the workers what to do. The honeybee workers, shown right, then take these chemicals and pass them from mouth to mouth through their proboscis. Bees also use this kind of communication to tell each other what sort of nectar is being produced by flowers near the hive.

Stab in the dark

In unclean conditions, bedbugs – like the one that is highly enlarged under the microscope, left – bite by night, causing swellings on the skin. Their mandibles and two of the palps form a sharp but delicate, pointed stabbing tube called a stylet. These parasites need a regular diet of blood and may bite with their stylets several times in succession.

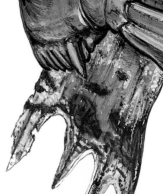

Antenna

Eye

Mandibles

Palps

Butterfly

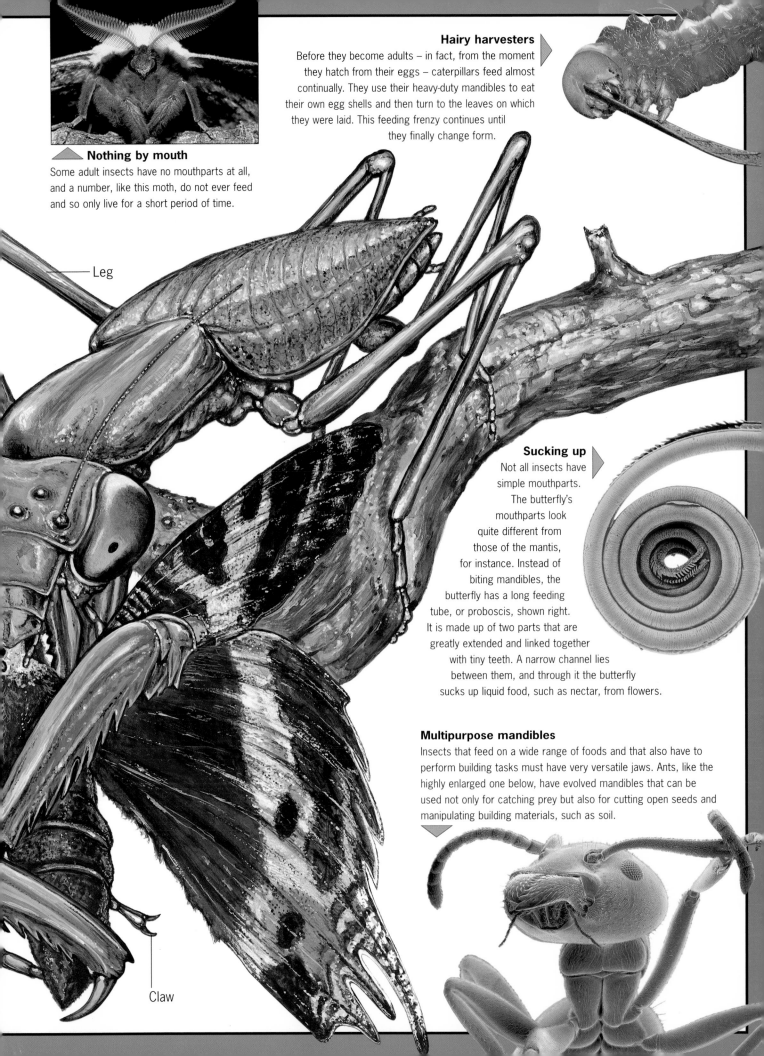

Hairy harvesters

Before they become adults – in fact, from the moment they hatch from their eggs – caterpillars feed almost continually. They use their heavy-duty mandibles to eat their own egg shells and then turn to the leaves on which they were laid. This feeding frenzy continues until they finally change form.

Nothing by mouth

Some adult insects have no mouthparts at all, and a number, like this moth, do not ever feed and so only live for a short period of time.

Leg

Sucking up

Not all insects have simple mouthparts. The butterfly's mouthparts look quite different from those of the mantis, for instance. Instead of biting mandibles, the butterfly has a long feeding tube, or proboscis, shown right. It is made up of two parts that are greatly extended and linked together with tiny teeth. A narrow channel lies between them, and through it the butterfly sucks up liquid food, such as nectar, from flowers.

Multipurpose mandibles

Insects that feed on a wide range of foods and that also have to perform building tasks must have very versatile jaws. Ants, like the highly enlarged one below, have evolved mandibles that can be used not only for catching prey but also for cutting open seeds and manipulating building materials, such as soil.

Claw

WING STRUCTURE

A young damselfly starts to take to the air. The previous day, it had left the water to climb up a reed, where it shed its nymphal exoskeleton. Then, as blood was pumped through the thinnest veins you can imagine that lie within its wings, these highly efficient organs of flight took shape. Despite their flimsy appearance, the damselfly's wings are capable of impressive aerobatics. In just a few feet it can go from full speed to a complete standstill.

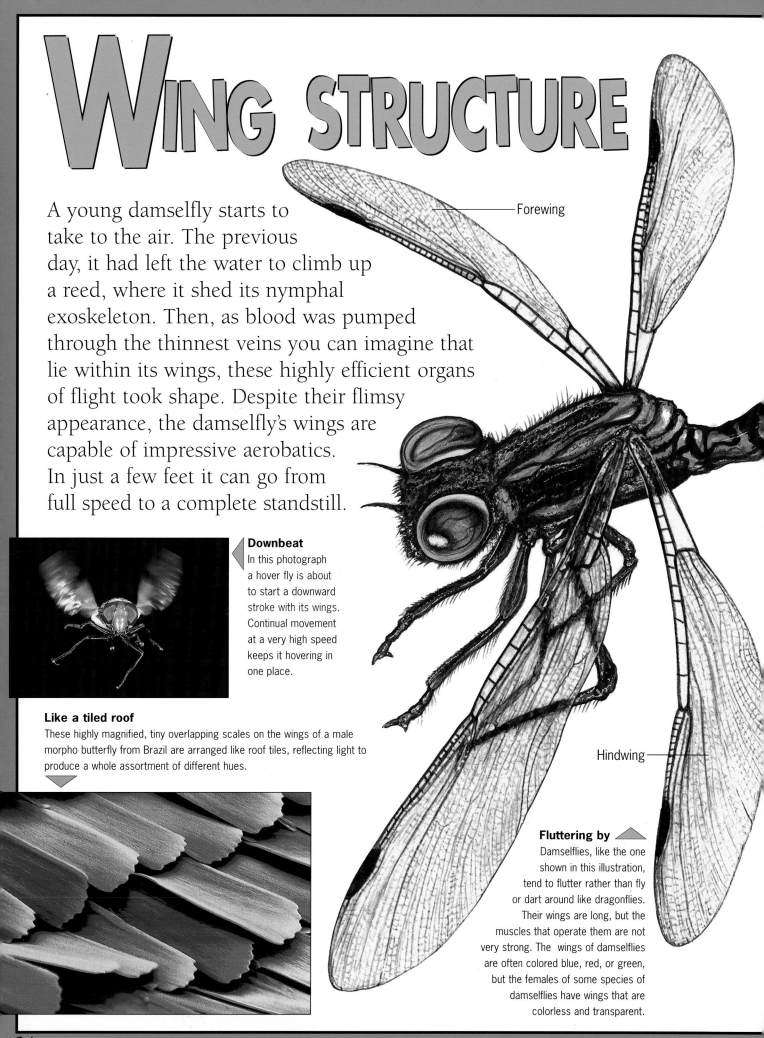

Forewing

Hindwing

Downbeat
In this photograph a hover fly is about to start a downward stroke with its wings. Continual movement at a very high speed keeps it hovering in one place.

Like a tiled roof
These highly magnified, tiny overlapping scales on the wings of a male morpho butterfly from Brazil are arranged like roof tiles, reflecting light to produce a whole assortment of different hues.

Fluttering by
Damselflies, like the one shown in this illustration, tend to flutter rather than fly or dart around like dragonflies. Their wings are long, but the muscles that operate them are not very strong. The wings of damselflies are often colored blue, red, or green, but the females of some species of damselflies have wings that are colorless and transparent.

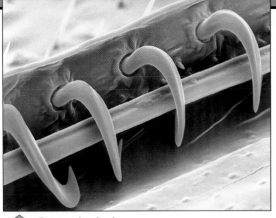

On the fringe
This gall-producing Cuban laurel thrip, a sap-sucker, has characteristic long fringes of hair on its four wings. In this photograph, it has been magnified to ten times life size.

— Abdomen

▲ **Dynamic design**
The hooklike structures on the edge of a honeybee's wings are used to couple them together to form a combined surface for flight.

One of the most obvious characteristics of many species of insects in their adult phase is the presence of one or two pairs of wings. In fact, without the ability to fly, insects would have been unable to colonize the world so quickly.

Their wings are made up of two layers of a strong, flexible substance known as *sclerotin*. Between the two layers run a number of toughened veins that lend support to the wings and also carry hemolymph, the insect's blood, which is pumped into the wings just after it matures so that they can expand to be used. Each species of insect has its own particular wing patterning that helps with identification.

Insect wings vary greatly in size. The wings of the tiny fairyfly wasp, for instance, are so small that they are hardly visible to the naked eye.

But the wingspan of one type of moth is highly impressive at 12 inches. Some very small insects that do not take to the air readily have fringed wings. They help them move with greater ease by acting much like the flaps on an airplane. Insects that fly rapidly, however, may have only one pair of wings instead of two. This is the case with flies. However, they have a specially adapted second pair, known as *halteres*, that help with balance.

Butterflies' wings are undoubtedly the most stunning of any insect wings. The colors of the scales covering them may be due to the diffraction of light or to body chemicals. Not only are there variations in wing shape in different species of butterflies, there may also be differences between the sexes in color and pattern.

On the spot
The two black and white eyespots on the hindwings of this South American butterfly are a mimicry device. Resembling the eyes of a larger animal, the spots are used to startle predators when the butterfly suddenly flashes its hind-wings at them.

Finely veined
This enlargement of part of the wing of a dragonfly clearly shows its fine veining. The wings themselves are delicate and gauzelike, but the patterning of veins helps keep them stiff and aids flight. Even when they are resting, dragonflies hold their magnificent wings outstretched.

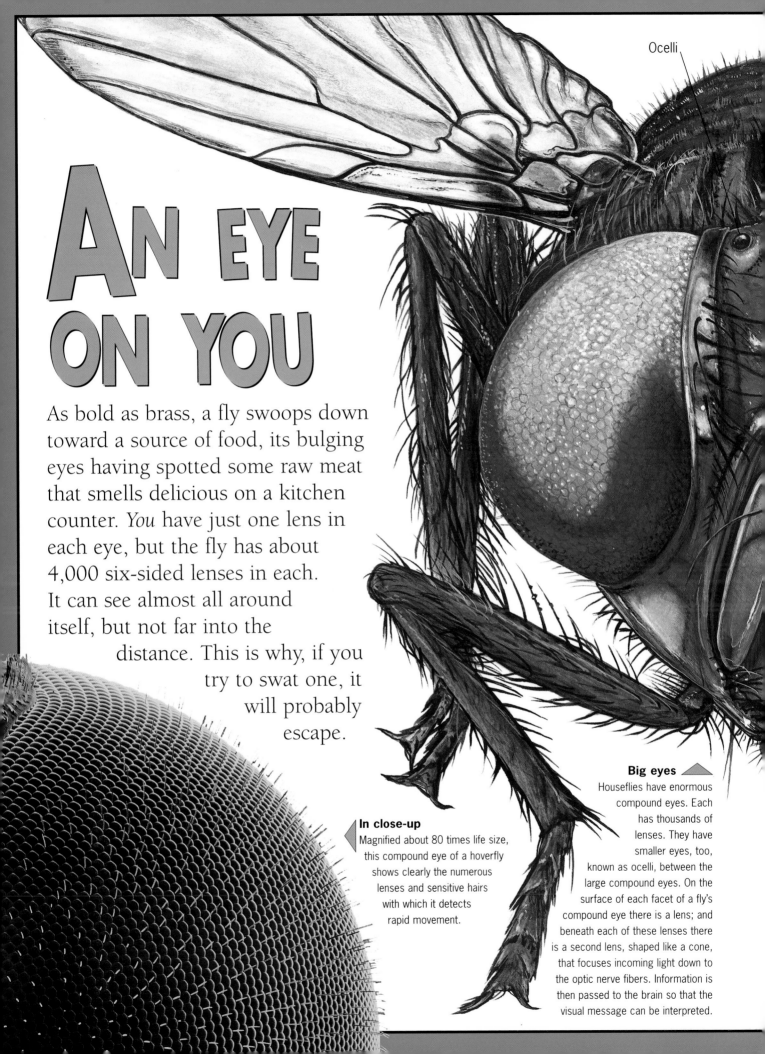

Ocelli

An eye on you

As bold as brass, a fly swoops down toward a source of food, its bulging eyes having spotted some raw meat that smells delicious on a kitchen counter. *You* have just one lens in each eye, but the fly has about 4,000 six-sided lenses in each. It can see almost all around itself, but not far into the distance. This is why, if you try to swat one, it will probably escape.

In close-up
Magnified about 80 times life size, this compound eye of a hoverfly shows clearly the numerous lenses and sensitive hairs with which it detects rapid movement.

Big eyes
Houseflies have enormous compound eyes. Each has thousands of lenses. They have smaller eyes, too, known as ocelli, between the large compound eyes. On the surface of each facet of a fly's compound eye there is a lens; and beneath each of these lenses there is a second lens, shaped like a cone, that focuses incoming light down to the optic nerve fibers. Information is then passed to the brain so that the visual message can be interpreted.

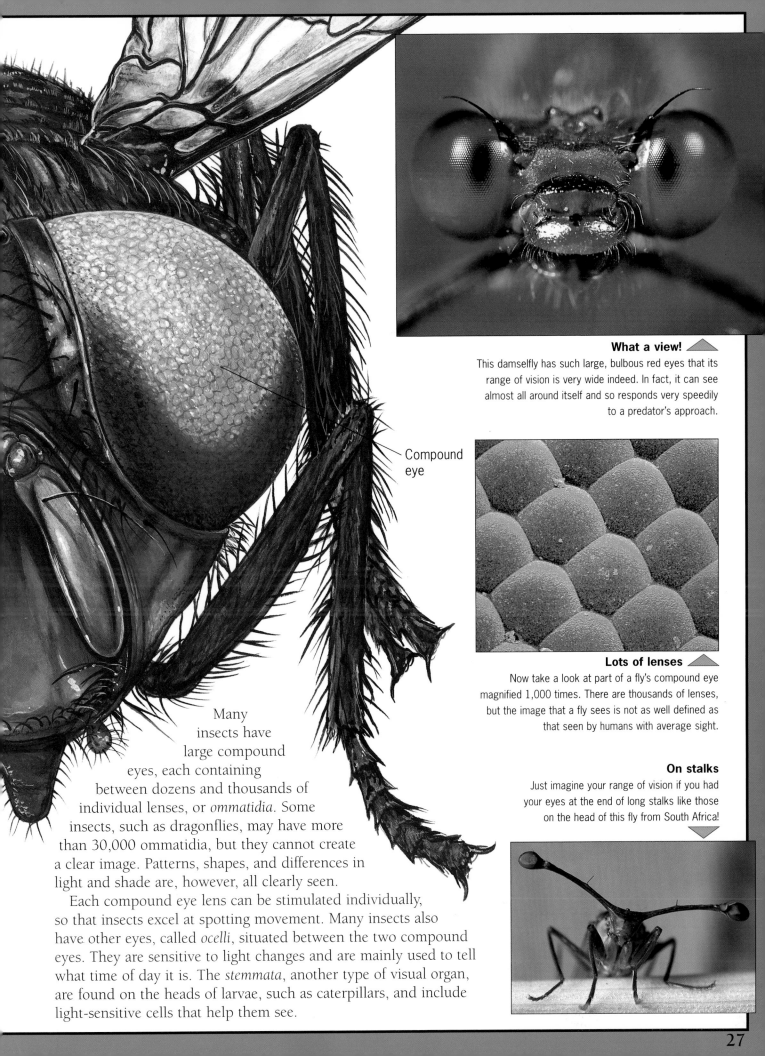

Compound
eye

Many
insects have
large compound
eyes, each containing
between dozens and thousands of
individual lenses, or *ommatidia*. Some
insects, such as dragonflies, may have more
than 30,000 ommatidia, but they cannot create
a clear image. Patterns, shapes, and differences in
light and shade are, however, all clearly seen.

Each compound eye lens can be stimulated individually,
so that insects excel at spotting movement. Many insects also
have other eyes, called *ocelli*, situated between the two compound
eyes. They are sensitive to light changes and are mainly used to tell
what time of day it is. The *stemmata*, another type of visual organ,
are found on the heads of larvae, such as caterpillars, and include
light-sensitive cells that help them see.

What a view!
This damselfly has such large, bulbous red eyes that its
range of vision is very wide indeed. In fact, it can see
almost all around itself and so responds very speedily
to a predator's approach.

Lots of lenses
Now take a look at part of a fly's compound eye
magnified 1,000 times. There are thousands of lenses,
but the image that a fly sees is not as well defined as
that seen by humans with average sight.

On stalks
Just imagine your range of vision if you had
your eyes at the end of long stalks like those
on the head of this fly from South Africa!

MAKING SOUNDS

A baby robin chances to land on a branch where a death's head hawkmoth caterpillar has been feeding greedily for a few hours. Immediately, the 4-inch-long larva starts to produce a series of loud clicks. Its aim is to startle the bird with this strange noise so that it can avoid ending up as the robin's prey.

Sound is used by some insects for several important reasons – to attract a mate or for self-defense, for example. But those insects that make sounds do not all produce them in the same way. Some have quite simple methods, while others need to put more complex mechanisms to use. One of the most common means of producing sound is *stridulation*, involving the scraping of one specialized part of the body, the *scraper*, against another part, called the *file*. The resulting sound can sometimes be quite loud.

Alarm signals

Most caterpillars are silent. But when a death's head hawk moth caterpillar is disturbed, it can produce some clicking sounds. They are not very loud but can be enough to take a predator completely by surprise.

Cryptic calls

The cryptic ambush bug in the photograph below is superbly camouflaged against rotting vegetation. It has a special chirping organ under its proboscis that it rubs against its thorax as an alarm if under attack.

Sweet serenades

Tree crickets, like the one framed by a partly eaten leaf in this photograph, make music to attract the opposite sex. Only male crickets stridulate and do this by rubbing their wings together. Their songs have a higher pitch than those of the grasshoppers.

Clickety-click

This large click beetle from the West Indies can throw itself up in the air to correct its stance if knocked over and will land with a loud clicking noise, made when a spine on the underside of the thorax is snapped into a groove.

When the scraper is dragged over the file, it makes a scratching sound. On its own this would not travel very far, so adaptations need to be made. To amplify the sound, insects use other body parts, including their wings and breathing tubes. They help project the sound over a considerable distance.

Another method of sound production calls for use of organs known as *tymbals*. Insects that make sounds in this way usually have their tymbals on either side of the thorax or abdomen. The tymbals are thin sheets of cuticle surrounded by muscles. As the muscles contract, the tymbals buckle and go pop. When the muscles relax, the tymbals relax and again make a popping noise. These muscles may contract hundreds of times each second, producing very strident sounds.

Knocking on wood

If you ever hear a loud tapping noise at night, it could be that death watch beetles have infested the timbers of your home or some of your furniture. It is the mating call of this species of beetle that sounds like this, as they bang their heads against the wood over and over again.

Singing along

This male meadow grasshopper is stridulating to attract a mate by rubbing a file on its front leg against a scraper on its forewing. This method of sound-production is different from the method used by katydids and crickets, which does not involve their legs.

29

HOMES

Just like all members of the animal kingdom, ourselves included, insects need homes in which to live. We might choose a house, an apartment, a trailer, or a boat. Insect abodes, however, are far more varied.

There are those, for example, that find it snug to live deep in the soil, while others form teams of thousands of their own kind to build what are the most amazing architectural wonders, many feet high and above ground. Some dwell in nests, or fashion webs of silk, or bore into dead wood. A few, meanwhile, are nomadic by nature and never stay for long in one place. How, though, does a wasp go about building its nest? Which insects share their homes with lodgers? What is it like inside termite towers? How do some insects spin their own homes? Open up to these and many other questions about insect homes as you enter the various types of dwelling described and illustrated on the pages that follow.

Home furnishings
Leaf-cutting bees, like the one shown here, remove portions from leaves with their strong mandibles and use the cuttings to line the cells in their nests.

Insect skyscrapers
Turn to pages 48-49 to discover which type of insect built this remarkable structure for its home. The mound is taller than a giraffe, and has an excellent airconditioning system.

Inside information
On pages 38-39, we invite you to watch as another insect prepares to lay its eggs in a very unusual place. When the larvae hatch, they will be right inside their food source.

Dangerous domiciles
Some plants are carnivorous – that is, they trap and eat any insects that try to make a home in them. You can find out all about such deathtrap housing on pages 42-43.

ARCHITECTURAL WONDERS

The internal structure of this wasp nest is made up of lots of papier mâché cells and is a magnificent piece of building work. The exterior of this type of paper wasp nest, meanwhile, both looks good and is very practical. It has just been finished, and the wasps have molded lots of spikes on the outside that will add valuable protection to their unique lightweight, but very strong premises. This is just one of a whole assortment of custom-built insect homes, constructed from materials as diverse as earth, mud, foam, foliage, saliva, wax, silk, and woodpulp. What splendid pieces of design some of these residences are!

Nests of mud
These two clay nests have been made by potter wasps. They are solitary insects, and the clay nest is their equivalent of the communal hive.

Rolling home
An oak-roller weevil is seen here on top of foliage that it has wound around and around. It can lay its eggs inside, and the hatching larvae will have a leaf on which to feed. They will emerge from the rolled leaf after pupating.

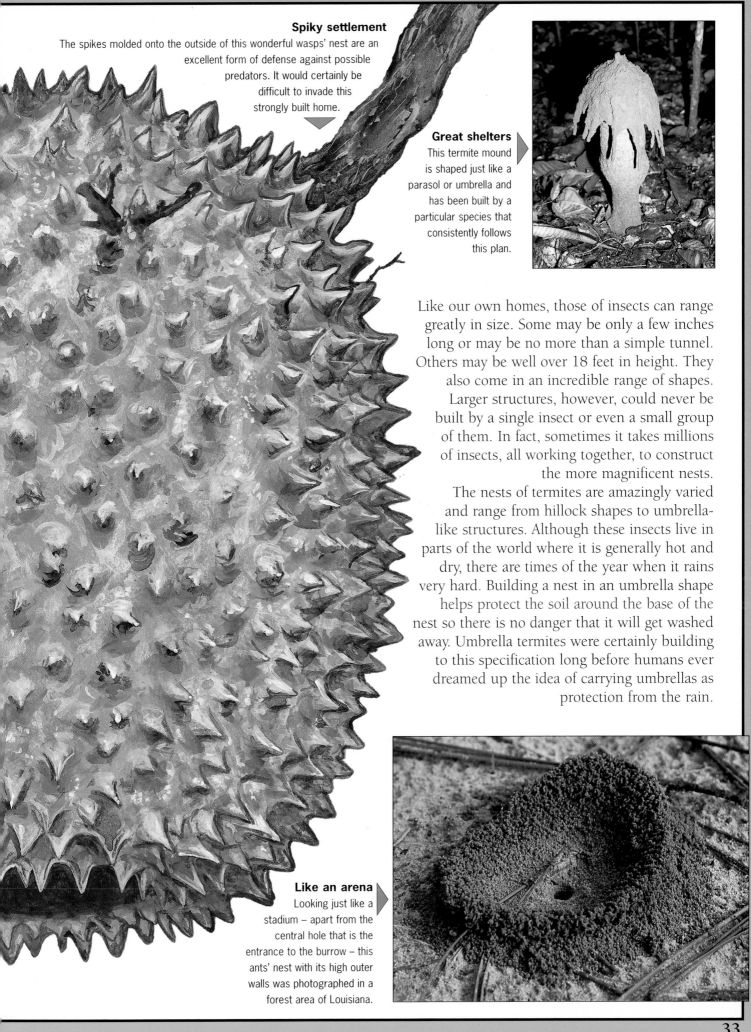

Spiky settlement
The spikes molded onto the outside of this wonderful wasps' nest are an excellent form of defense against possible predators. It would certainly be difficult to invade this strongly built home.

Great shelters
This termite mound is shaped just like a parasol or umbrella and has been built by a particular species that consistently follows this plan.

Like our own homes, those of insects can range greatly in size. Some may be only a few inches long or may be no more than a simple tunnel. Others may be well over 18 feet in height. They also come in an incredible range of shapes. Larger structures, however, could never be built by a single insect or even a small group of them. In fact, sometimes it takes millions of insects, all working together, to construct the more magnificent nests.

The nests of termites are amazingly varied and range from hillock shapes to umbrella-like structures. Although these insects live in parts of the world where it is generally hot and dry, there are times of the year when it rains very hard. Building a nest in an umbrella shape helps protect the soil around the base of the nest so there is no danger that it will get washed away. Umbrella termites were certainly building to this specification long before humans ever dreamed up the idea of carrying umbrellas as protection from the rain.

Like an arena
Looking just like a stadium – apart from the central hole that is the entrance to the burrow – this ants' nest with its high outer walls was photographed in a forest area of Louisiana.

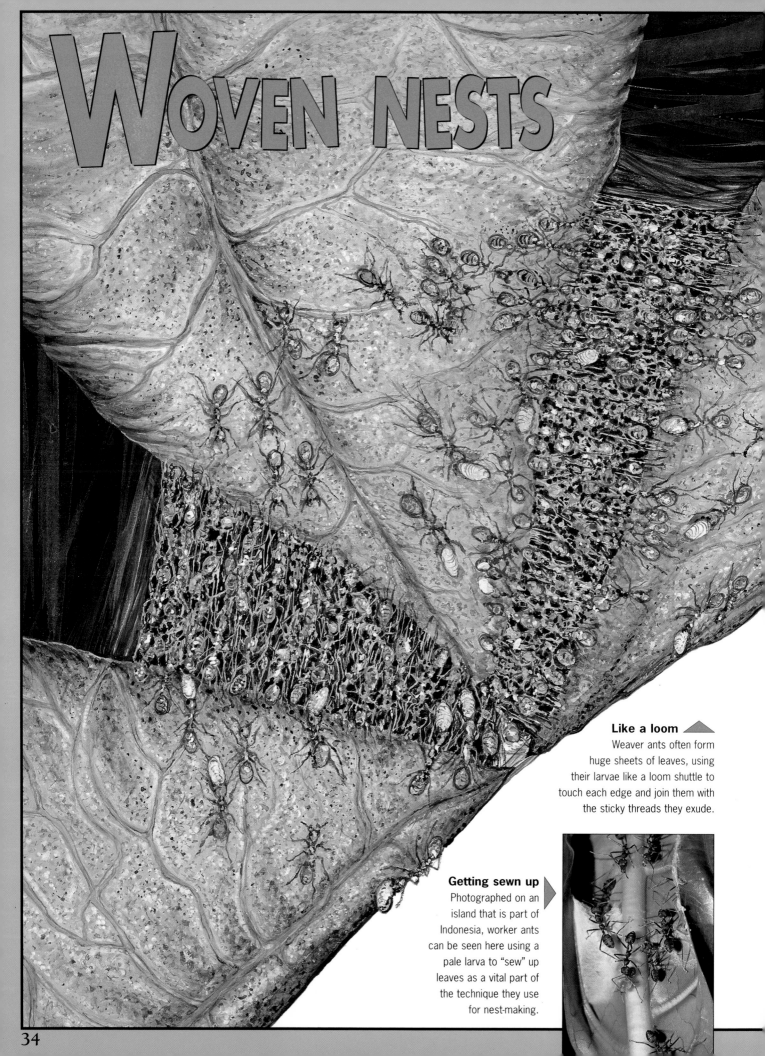

WOVEN NESTS

Like a loom
Weaver ants often form huge sheets of leaves, using their larvae like a loom shuttle to touch each edge and join them with the sticky threads they exude.

Getting sewn up
Photographed on an island that is part of Indonesia, worker ants can be seen here using a pale larva to "sew" up leaves as a vital part of the technique they use for nest-making.

In among the foliage of a forest in India hundreds of weaver ants are busy as they cooperate on the construction of nests of leaves. To assist with this, they need additional help and will call on their larvae as sources of silk with which to bind the foliage together. With remarkable speed and efficiency the nests begin to take form and will soon be completed.

Ants are well known for joining forces and working hard as a unit. So it should come as no surprise to learn that in Sri Lanka, India, Papua New Guinea, Australia, and Africa even the young of certain species of ants have an important role to play in nest-building. A first generation is allowed to mature outside a nest; and when they are ready, the workers will be able to assist with feeding a further batch of grubs. The mature workers then put their young charges to good use as nest-building proceeds.

YOUNG ASSISTANTS

Once the grubs are ready to spin their cocoons, their silk glands will be exploited. Mature ants cannot spin silk, and so they must rely on the brood. First, a number of workers will hold two leaves so that they form a tentlike shape. Some may even make a living chain by grasping each other and pulling together, like one side of a tug of war. Several workers will then each carry a larva to the edges of the leaves. Each larva is then made to touch the surface with its head so that it produces a small amount of liquid silk. Individual larvae will next be lifted and taken to the edge of the other leaf so that the gumlike fluid that is secreted will stick the leaves together. The nest will be a strong structure, sometimes extending to one foot in diameter, and will provide adequate shelter for the growing colony.

Pulling together
Two weaver ants can be seen here, cooperating closely as they both hold together a leaf in its rolled form. Without such communal effort, their nests could never be constructed. Ants are in fact a prime example of social insects, living together and working as a team. The whole colony benefits as a result.

Spinning a home
This web-spinner, photographed in Trinidad, lives inside the silken galleries that it spins by using the glands on its forelegs. Its woven nest is usually built on moss or in the soil.

Weavers at work
Photographed in Australia, these worker ants and the brood are about to begin their sewing. If, as it is often said, the use of tools is a sign of intelligence, then use of their larvae as tools to join leaves together could be a sign of the high intelligence of ants.

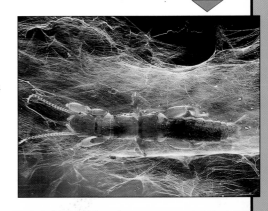

SAFE HOUSES

An adult silkworm moth has just emerged from the snug cocoon in which it has been living during its final developmental stage. Earlier in its lifecycle, over a period of days, it built this home by spinning a structure of threads, possibly almost a mile long in all. The resulting cocoon looks soft and comfortable; and its color may be cream, yellow, or even a pale hue of green according to the species. In captivity a silkworm would be lucky to reach this stage. Silkworm producers who farm them for profit usually kill the developing chrysalis inside the cocoon.

Snug in a cell
This section through a cell in the nest of a paper wasp shows an infertile adult female worker in the process of metamorphosis. She matures six weeks after the egg has been laid.

A cozy home
The moth caterpillar above has started to spin the secure cocoon in which it will undergo complete metamorphosis.

A silkworm's shelter is known as a cocoon, and the threads from which it is made are secreted by special glands. The threads, if extended, would measure up to seven times the silkworm's body length. Curiously, a silkworm that will develop into a female moth has longer silk glands than one that will become a male. Wrapping the threads all around its form may take the silkworm several thousand shakes of its head, but it is worthwhile because, inside, it will be safe and sound. In fact, the cocoon of a domestic silkworm is so secure that it becomes a kind of prison. The cocoons of wild silkmoths, however, are not nearly so tough. Many other insects also spend an early part of their lives developing inside cocoons – some species of meadow ants, for instance, lacewings, and some wasps.

Structures of silk
Silkworm caterpillars feed greedily and then spin frameworks of silk in which they remain safely tucked away and can pupate.

Leaving home
The silk moth in the picture below has emerged from its cocoon and is stretching its wings. It was not raised on a silk farm and so was not killed in its chrysalis by exposure to very high temperatures. Instead, it was left to mature.

Open house
In the photograph above, a mulberry silk moth cocoon has been cut open to show the pupa and the skin from its last molt.

37

Lots of insects build their houses in trees, but sometimes it is the tree itself that grows homes for them. You may have noticed swellings on branches at times. They are galls, and inside them larvae of various kinds are probably to be found. Galls come in many shapes, colors, and sizes.

SWELL PLACE

Inside a gall

In the photograph below, a section has been cut through a gall to show the developing wasp larva that is well protected inside it.

Deep inside a few swellings on the outside of an oak tree wasp larvae are feeding. As a response to their presence some of the tree's cells have multiplied in size and number to produce structures that will both protect the larvae while they mature to adulthood and provide a source of nourishment. *Galls*, as these growths are known, may appear on roots, leaves, twigs, or branches. At first they are green, but they turn red or brown with time and may grow to the size of a large apple.

Meet the occupant
An entomologist has cut through the oak gall above so that you can see the live wasp that has been growing inside the round swelling.

Pea-dwellers
These pea galls, named because of their shape, are growing on the leaves of a rose bush. They were formed in response to the presence of some wasp larvae.

A hop-shaped home
The gall that has formed here is shaped like a hop plant and has grown around a particular species of wasp. Entomologists can readily identify the species from the shape of the gall.

Among the strangest insect homes of all are those in which the gall insects live. However, these insects do not build their own homes. Instead, they manage to trick certain plants into doing all the building work for them.

When the larva of a gall-producing insect hatches, it starts to feed almost immediately. At the same time, it produces special chemicals in its saliva, droppings, and other bodily secretions. They have the effect of making the plant cells grow in a specific way so that swellings occur. Within a short time the developing swellings, or galls, will entirely surround the young insects, providing a safe haven.

SHAPING UP

Each species of gall-producing insect creates its own distinctively shaped gall from which it will eventually have to emerge through an excavated tunnel. The form of the gall depends on several factors, but most often it is the way in which an insect feeds that influences the gall's appearance.

Beetles, caterpillars, and wasps, for instance, feed using their jaws, and the physical damage they do affects the shape of their galls.

Bugs and flies usually have piercing mouthparts that cause less damage to a plant and a different form of gall. In fact, it is sometimes the shape of the gall that will help identify the insect.

Strangely, one gall wasp from California gives birth to two very different generations each year. The eggs of the first – produced parthenogenetically and including females only – occur in stem galls of one type of oak; and the eggs of the second batch – produced sexually and including both males and females – are found in the leaf galls of a different type of oak.

LOATHSOME LODGERS

The vilest of visitors

The cockroaches above are gathering at a table that was left uncleared overnight. They will feast on the sandwich and other spilled crumbs, as well as liquids.

Filthy flies

Houseflies, like the one shown at high magnification below, spread germs and are therefore unwelcome in our homes. They may land on animal excrement one minute and fly into the kitchen the next.

John's room is usually quite a noisy place as he listens to his radio, plays computer games, or watches TV. But even when he is not at home, or at night when he is asleep, there may be considerable activity going on. A few tenants may have set up home in his rug, others could have occupied a corner of the loft, some might even have taken up residence in his cozy bed, and one or two of his books might be providing a hideout for certain minuscule lodgers who have crept in unnoticed.

Holes in the carpet, a few wasps spotted entering or leaving a roof area, a peculiar odor after leaving food around overnight, red marks on your body, chewed corners to the pages of a book – all may be signs that there are various forms of infestation in your home. The pantry, though, is the most likely place to find such invaders as mealworms, weevils, beetles, and cockroaches. But these lodgers are not only loathed for the obvious damage they cause and the food they defile; some people may actually be allergic to contact with their waste. It has even been suggested that some supposed food allergies could turn out to be cockroach related because of the frequency with which these pests infest our food.

Under the covers

This bedbug, shown in an enlarged photomicrograph, needs a regular diet of blood and feeds at night on sleeping victims, producing swellings on the skin as it bites. A victim will usually find that these itch terribly.

In the rafters

Wasps sometimes move indoors and build their nests in unused attics or lofts. If that happens, it will be necessary to call in the pest controllers to remove the nest. Never try to do this yourself. You risk being stung badly by the wasps as they try to defend their home.

Inside pages

The booklouse below has been photographed as it walks over the small type of a printed page. These lice sometimes get into books that are damp or not often read or dusted, and like to feed on any mold that forms on the paper.

Rascals in the rug

The carpet beetle larvae in the photograph above are also known as wooly bears. It is not hard to guess why! They may look cute and fluffy, but they attack fabrics and stored food, and have voracious appetites.

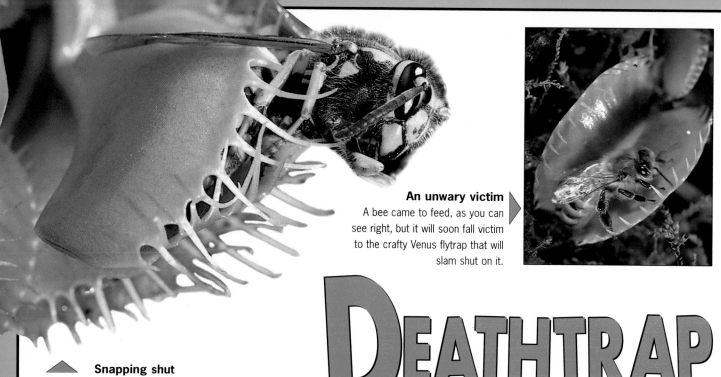

An unwary victim
A bee came to feed, as you can see right, but it will soon fall victim to the crafty Venus flytrap that will slam shut on it.

DEATHTRAP HOUSING

Snapping shut
The Venus flytrap is not particular about the type of insects that it catches, in spite of its name. In the photograph above, for example, it has entrapped a wasp. There is no chance that the insect will be able to get away from this carnivorous plant.

On the lookout for food, a fly peeks over the slippery edge of a brightly colored pitcher plant. Meanwhile, swimming around in the water that has collected deep inside, a whole variety of carnivorous insects awaits the arrival of another unfortunate victim that will almost certainly fall in and join them. The fly does eventually lose its footing, in spite of a strong grip, and downward-facing hairs on the plant prevent its escape. Having drowned, the fly will soon be eaten by the hungry swimmers. Their droppings will in turn nourish the plant.

The sly sundew
Lots of insects get caught by sundew plants and find that they cannot get free from their sticky surfaces. For the ant below there is trouble in store as it fights to escape. It is unlikely to be successful and so will die there.

A sticky end
The sundew plant below has also brought a victim to a sticky end. This time it is a fly that has got stuck, and the plant will soon curl around it. The sundew is not a good spot for an insect to choose as a resting place.

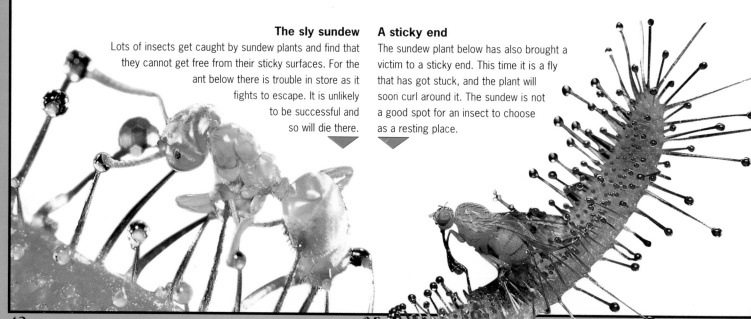

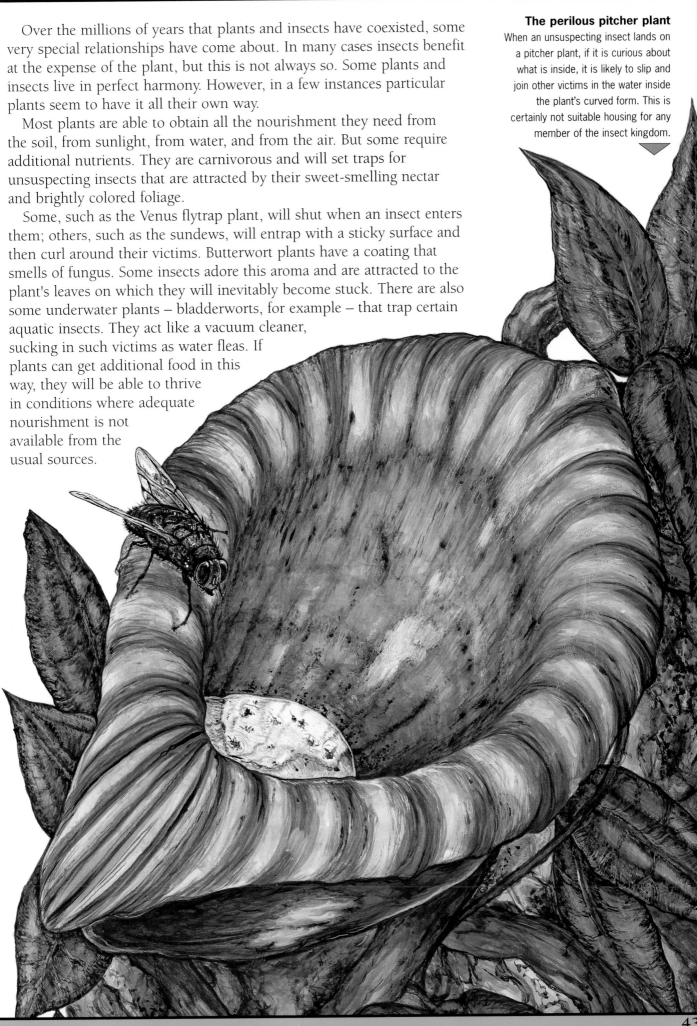

Over the millions of years that plants and insects have coexisted, some very special relationships have come about. In many cases insects benefit at the expense of the plant, but this is not always so. Some plants and insects live in perfect harmony. However, in a few instances particular plants seem to have it all their own way.

Most plants are able to obtain all the nourishment they need from the soil, from sunlight, from water, and from the air. But some require additional nutrients. They are carnivorous and will set traps for unsuspecting insects that are attracted by their sweet-smelling nectar and brightly colored foliage.

Some, such as the Venus flytrap plant, will shut when an insect enters them; others, such as the sundews, will entrap with a sticky surface and then curl around their victims. Butterwort plants have a coating that smells of fungus. Some insects adore this aroma and are attracted to the plant's leaves on which they will inevitably become stuck. There are also some underwater plants – bladderworts, for example – that trap certain aquatic insects. They act like a vacuum cleaner, sucking in such victims as water fleas. If plants can get additional food in this way, they will be able to thrive in conditions where adequate nourishment is not available from the usual sources.

The perilous pitcher plant
When an unsuspecting insect lands on a pitcher plant, if it is curious about what is inside, it is likely to slip and join other victims in the water inside the plant's curved form. This is certainly not suitable housing for any member of the insect kingdom.

43

PAPER HOUSES

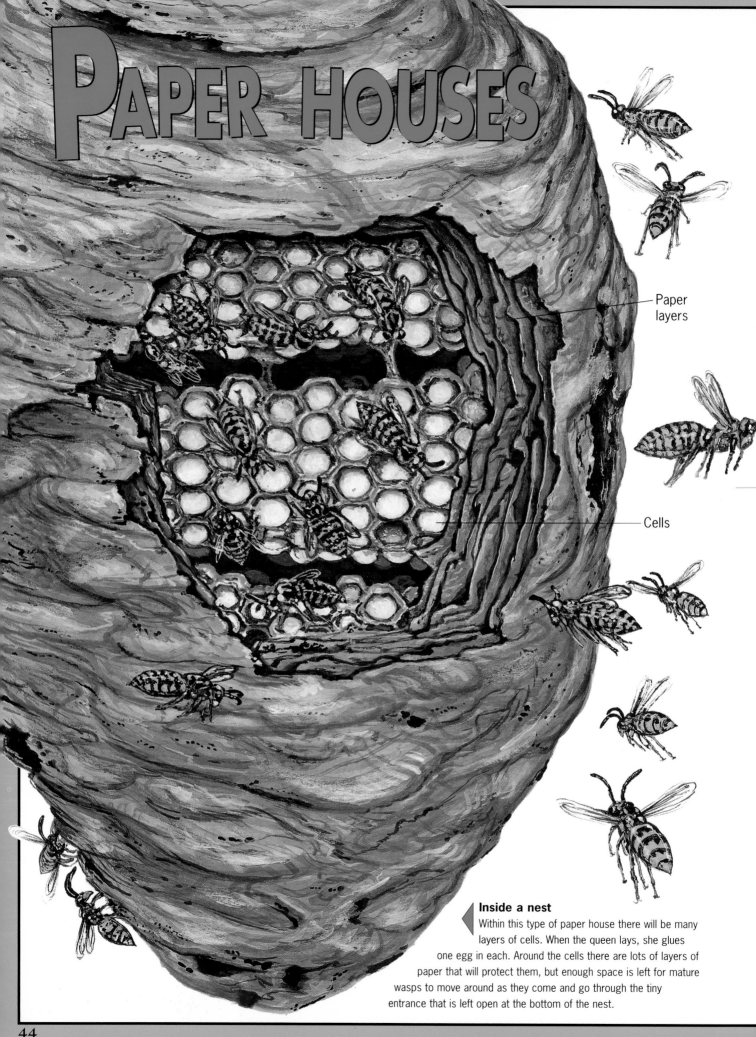

Paper
layers

Cells

Inside a nest
Within this type of paper house there will be many
layers of cells. When the queen lays, she glues
one egg in each. Around the cells there are lots of layers of
paper that will protect them, but enough space is left for mature
wasps to move around as they come and go through the tiny
entrance that is left open at the bottom of the nest.

Usually there is only a tiny entrance at the bottom of the nest, which is easy to guard, and which helps prevent the colony from becoming overheated in the height of summer. But in the illustration, *left*, part of the side of a paper wasps' nest has been cut away to reveal the structure of the interior – something it would normally not be safe to do. If disturbed in this way, the wasps would be sure to sting like crazy. Inside, as you can see, there are lots of six-sided cells, in each of which an egg may be laid. Young queens are responsible for starting such fabulous paper structures.

Nest-building
The European paper wasp above has just started to construct a nest. It will be smaller than the nests of most other social wasps, with under 100 cells.

A wasp queen will need a safe place in which to raise her large family and first looks for a suitable spot. It could be in a tree or even the roof of a house. The nest will be made from a paper-like substance. The queen manufactures it herself by chewing up wood pulp to produce a lightweight material that provides good insulation. But first she must build a narrow stalk from which will hang a cap containing hexagonal (six-sided) cells of a uniform size. The queen measures them with her antennae. They will be the nurseries, and in each the queen will lay an egg.

Six-sided cells
These six-sided cells are part of a paper wasps' nest. They are built from wood scrapings taken from trees and fenceposts.

LOTS OF LAYERS
Around this basic structure the queen now begins to form the curved walls of the nest by building up layer on layer of the paper substance. Between these layers air becomes trapped, helping keep the temperature stable inside. Once the eggs have hatched, the queen will bring insects and nectar on which the larvae can feed, entering the nest through a tiny entrance. Its small size helps prevent the atmosphere in the nest from becoming too humid and keeps out predators. Soon the paper nest will be home to several thousand wasps – workers, drones, and new queens among them. Watching a wasps' nest of this type being built is even said to have provided the inspiration for paper-making to an ancient Chinese observer.

Making a home
The hornet in the photograph shown on the right is busy cutting wood. It will reduce it to pulp and use it for building a nest.

A BORING LIFE

Tunnel-dweller
The stag beetle larva above has been photographed in a tunnel excavated in a rotting oak stump. It will feed continually on the wood.

Slowly, but with immense strength for such small insects, the tough jaws of a group of longhorn beetle larvae cut their way through the dead wood of a fallen tree. As splinters of wood are pushed into their mouths, the soft white bodies wriggle forward a few fractions of an inch until their jaws are again pressed against the wood. Slowly they open their jaws once more and bite into the wood again, just as they have done day in and day out for many years. Eventually it is time to pupate.

An edible home
Some beetle larvae develop inside wood and eat away at their environment as they slowly bore their way along. They may spend a great many years leading this "boring" life before pupating there.

Leaf tracks

These odd tracks inside a leaf were made by the caterpillar of a moth as it fed from rainforest vegetation in Costa Rica.

The main activity among most insects that have a larval stage is eating. So what better way for a grub to ensure that it gets enough to develop to maturity than to set up home *inside* its food! Those insects that live in food with a high nutrient level generally have a short larval stage. Some flesh-eating maggots or fruit-eating caterpillars can complete this stage of their lives in a week. However, at the other extreme the larvae of a few wood-boring insects may take almost half a century to reach adulthood. Wood is sometimes not very nutritious, and so the larvae have to eat a lot of it.

BETWEEN THE LAYERS

Some insects can burrow into the smallest places to make a home. The caterpillar of the leaf-mining moth, for instance, will burrow between the actual layers of a leaf. You would not know it had been there but for the telltale wiggly brown trail they leave behind them.

It is not always wood or leaves, however, into which insects may bore. If you have ever bitten into an apple and found it bad, it could be that a codlin moth larva had tunneled to the center. Fortunately, apples that have been infested in this way will almost always fall to the ground before they are fully ripened and so will not be picked for eating.

Inside an acorn

Weevils, such as the one shown here as it withdraws its proboscis from an acorn, will lay their eggs inside plants. When the larvae hatch, they feed inside their home and pupate there, too.

SKYSCRAPER-BUILDERS

If you have ever walked down New York's Fifth Avenue, you will know how it feels to gaze up and feel completely dwarfed by the huge buildings. But the towers that termites construct can be far larger in proportion to their body size than any man-made skyscrapers are to us. What is more, they vary in shape a great deal. The tallest may even take 50 years to complete. Within them are indoor gardens, nurseries, yard after yard of twisting cement-lined tunnels, and the queen's special chamber.

Indoor gardens
Inside an opened termite mound in Botswana, immature termites are eating from the fungus garden that the older generation has prepared. It provides all the nourishment they need to complete their growth.

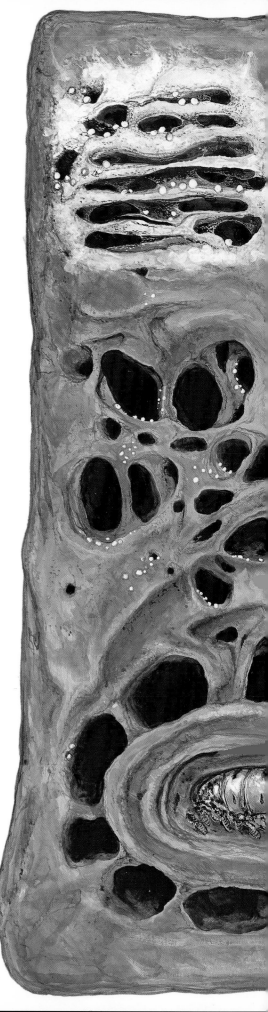

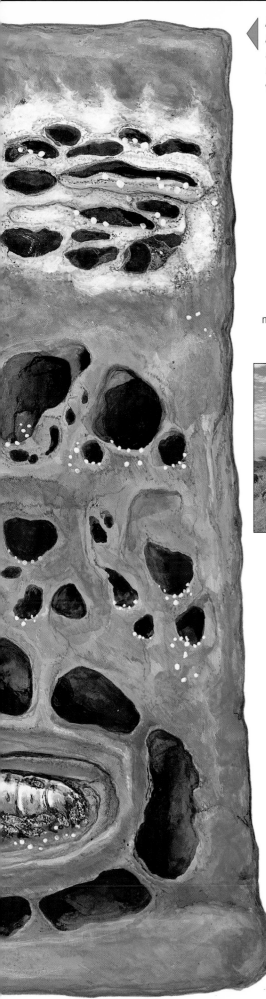

◄ **Above and below ground**
As well as the structure above ground, there are also passages that spread outward below the surface so the termites can forage for food without having to go into the open.

Massive mounds ►
This huge structure, called a cathedral termite mound because of its shape, is over 20 feet tall and well over three times the height of an average adult man. It was photographed in the Northern Territory of Australia.

Like a mountain
This odd ridged structure is not part of the natural bleak landscape of a distant planet. It is a termite mound, built right here on earth by millions of these tiny insects in one huge communal effort.

When explorers first went to Africa, they met with the most extraordinary sight. Spread out over the plains were huge, strangely shaped towers that seemed to have been constructed from earth. Which tribes had built these mounds, they wondered, and what was their purpose? When they tried to open them to see what was inside, they were astonished to find nothing but hordes of tiny, pale-colored creatures. These were not monuments after all but a most bizarre type of insect house.

MILLIONS OF RESIDENTS

Sometimes taller than a fully-grown giraffe and with strong walls built from mud and saliva, the mounds of the African termite are awesome structures. As high as they are above ground, most of these nests are nevertheless buried below the surface. These multi-chambered insect skyscrapers are in fact among the most amazing feats of engineering in the whole of the insect kingdom. Looking like mushrooms or wigwams in some instances, they often have several million residents. One type of termite even makes a flat mound that points north-south, which is how it gets the common name of compass termite. It is an alignment that helps prevent overheating in the intense midday sun.

Termite mounds may be so enormous that if land is being cleared for farming or housing, it is sometimes necessary to remove them with explosives. A bulldozer simply is not strong enough.

NO HOME OF THEIR OWN

A bold female cuckoo wasp waits at the entrance to the nest of another species of wasp. When one eventually appears, the cuckoo will probably sting and kill it outright. What bravado! This cool customer will then proceed to enter her victim's nest. Here she will help herself to wax that she will use to construct cells. Inside them she will lay her eggs. Her young will be well provided for, but at the expense of others; for as soon as the cuckoo wasp has laid, she will leave the adopted nest forever and abandon the next generation.

House theft
Cuckoo wasps, like the one in the illustration shown left, are social parasites. They lay their eggs, just as the cuckoo bird does, in the nests of others and then wander off. The young are left to be reared by other worker wasps, who always seem to help out and never evict the strangers.

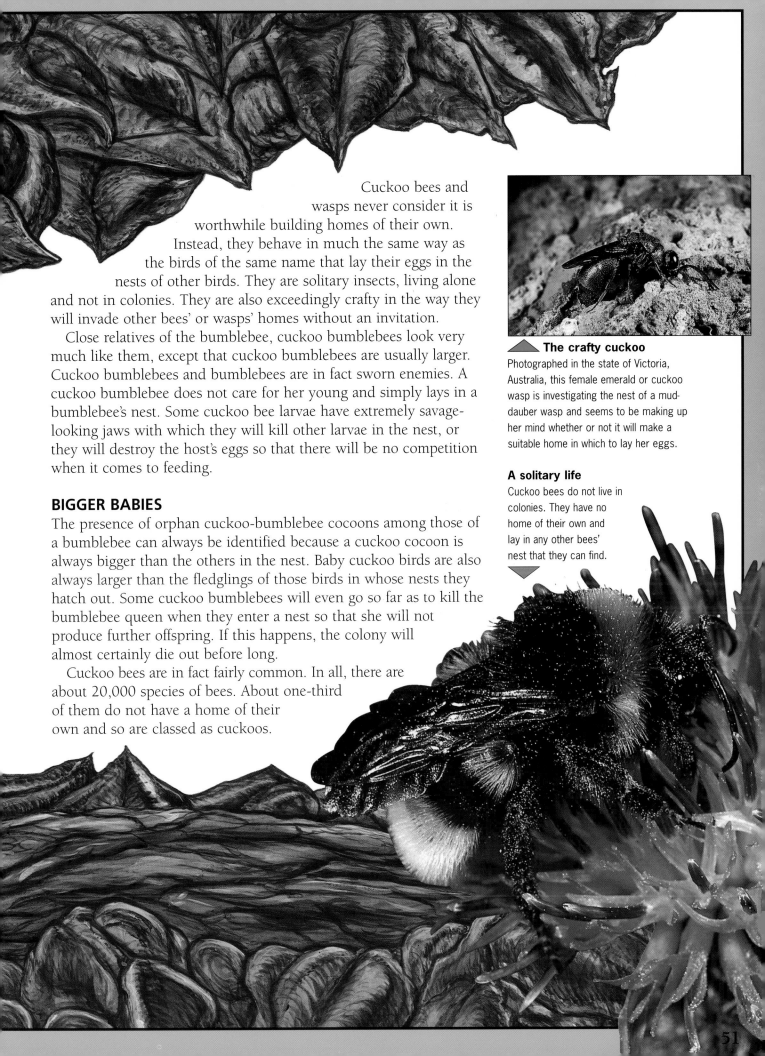

Cuckoo bees and wasps never consider it is worthwhile building homes of their own. Instead, they behave in much the same way as the birds of the same name that lay their eggs in the nests of other birds. They are solitary insects, living alone and not in colonies. They are also exceedingly crafty in the way they will invade other bees' or wasps' homes without an invitation.

Close relatives of the bumblebee, cuckoo bumblebees look very much like them, except that cuckoo bumblebees are usually larger. Cuckoo bumblebees and bumblebees are in fact sworn enemies. A cuckoo bumblebee does not care for her young and simply lays in a bumblebee's nest. Some cuckoo bee larvae have extremely savage-looking jaws with which they will kill other larvae in the nest, or they will destroy the host's eggs so that there will be no competition when it comes to feeding.

BIGGER BABIES

The presence of orphan cuckoo-bumblebee cocoons among those of a bumblebee can always be identified because a cuckoo cocoon is always bigger than the others in the nest. Baby cuckoo birds are also always larger than the fledglings of those birds in whose nests they hatch out. Some cuckoo bumblebees will even go so far as to kill the bumblebee queen when they enter a nest so that she will not produce further offspring. If this happens, the colony will almost certainly die out before long.

Cuckoo bees are in fact fairly common. In all, there are about 20,000 species of bees. About one-third of them do not have a home of their own and so are classed as cuckoos.

The crafty cuckoo
Photographed in the state of Victoria, Australia, this female emerald or cuckoo wasp is investigating the nest of a mud-dauber wasp and seems to be making up her mind whether or not it will make a suitable home in which to lay her eggs.

A solitary life
Cuckoo bees do not live in colonies. They have no home of their own and lay in any other bees' nest that they can find.

51

LIFESTYLES

Behavior in the insect kingdom varies considerably from species to species. Many are miniature thieves, night-prowlers, trap-setters, mimics, or even cannibals. In complete contrast, some are caring and self-sacrificing, living in colonies and working in teams to ensure the survival of their community. Did you know, for instance, that some types of male mosquitoes will perform a special dance to attract a female before mating; that a great many insects excel at playing hide-and-seek; that some can spray venom; that a number seem to eat nonstop; and that others are highly aggressive? Insects were among the earliest inhabitants of the earth, having evolved over 400 million years ago, long before human beings first appeared. Most of their behavior patterns – such as swarming, trying to keep clean, scavenging, or migrating – are inborn, but a few insects seem capable of learning new things. Within the pages of this volume you will find revealed the many secrets of their success.

A great pretender

Not all insects are what they seem. Some mimic each other, and others look just like the vegetation in which they live. On pages 56-57, we present some of the great pretenders. You may not recognize them for what they are at first.

Busy bees

Enter the world of the honeybee on pages 60-61, and find out why they are always so busy, what it is like inside a hive, how they feed, and how all the members of the colony cooperate.

Making contact

Some insects, such as this butterfly, display their magnificent wings to attract a mate. Others make contact through sound or perfume trails. Glowworms and other bioluminescent insects use light signals, and some flies present their partners with nuptial gifts, as part of their mating games.

More than a snack

Which insects have the largest appetites? At what stage of their lives do some of them eat the most? What sort of diet do different insects enjoy? And is it true that some mature insects do not eat solid food but only drink? Find out as we look at insect eating habits on pages 58-59.

CHALLENGES

A tiger beetle has just launched an attack; but instead of submitting to defeat, the victim carpenter ant suddenly starts to shower this predatory creature with sticky goo. It is a rare phenomenon but a very effective one.

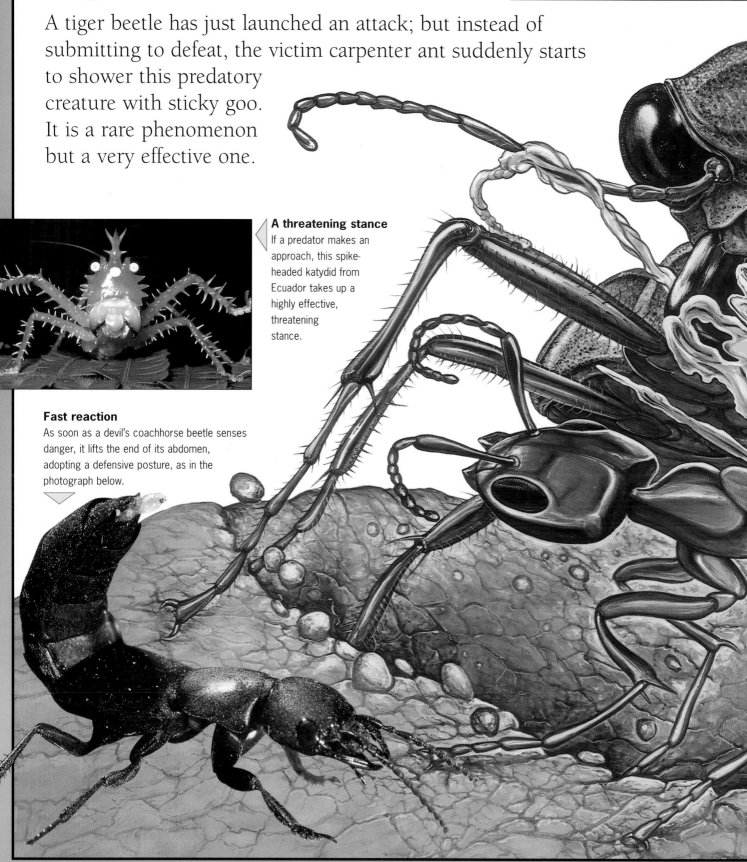

A threatening stance
If a predator makes an approach, this spike-headed katydid from Ecuador takes up a highly effective, threatening stance.

Fast reaction
As soon as a devil's coachhorse beetle senses danger, it lifts the end of its abdomen, adopting a defensive posture, as in the photograph below.

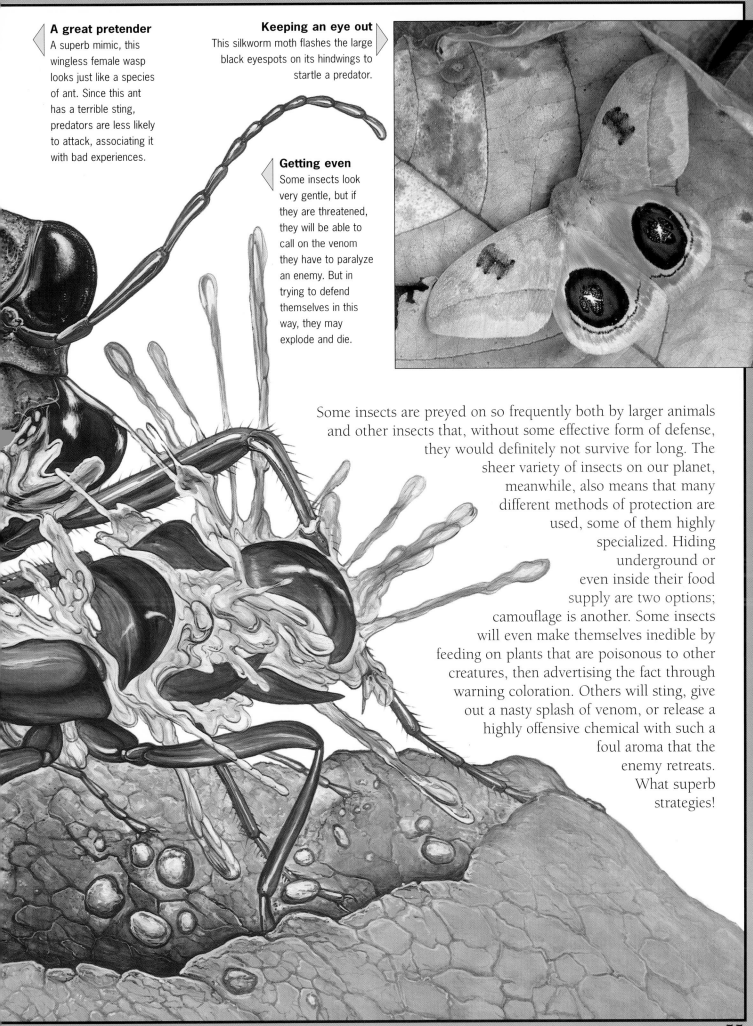

A great pretender
A superb mimic, this wingless female wasp looks just like a species of ant. Since this ant has a terrible sting, predators are less likely to attack, associating it with bad experiences.

Keeping an eye out
This silkworm moth flashes the large black eyespots on its hindwings to startle a predator.

Getting even
Some insects look very gentle, but if they are threatened, they will be able to call on the venom they have to paralyze an enemy. But in trying to defend themselves in this way, they may explode and die.

Some insects are preyed on so frequently both by larger animals and other insects that, without some effective form of defense, they would definitely not survive for long. The sheer variety of insects on our planet, meanwhile, also means that many different methods of protection are used, some of them highly specialized. Hiding underground or even inside their food supply are two options; camouflage is another. Some insects will even make themselves inedible by feeding on plants that are poisonous to other creatures, then advertising the fact through warning coloration. Others will sting, give out a nasty splash of venom, or release a highly offensive chemical with such a foul aroma that the enemy retreats. What superb strategies!

MIMICRY

A small monkey is completely taken aback. About to grab his lunch, he finds that the scrumptious-looking hawk moth caterpillar's head has suddenly taken on the form of a venomous snake! Clearly, being able to pretend to be something that a predator fears is a very useful talent.

Quick-change artist
Could it really be a snake, or is it merely a caterpillar that mimics one when it wants to frighten off an enemy that might eat it?

Snail-impersonator
Look carefully at this photograph, and you should be able to spot the sawfly larva that is lying on the ground. It seems to be masquerading as one of a cluster of snails.

The cheating fly
The tropical stilt-legged fly from the rainforest of South America in the photograph shown here tricks its enemies into believing it will deliver a harmful bite or sting because it looks so much like an ant. This is an excellent example of Batesian mimicry.

Leaf lookalikes
The leaf insect, left, was photographed in the Malaysian rainforest. It so closely resembles a leaf and keeps so still that from only a few feet away, it is completely unrecognizable as a life form. Predators will therefore entirely overlook it.

Caterpillar mimic
This North American caterpillar has brightly colored spikes that make it look like a poisonous animal or toxic plant. This usually keeps predators at bay because they associate these features with distasteful flesh.

False information
By mimicking a wasp and becoming deliberately conspicuous, this yellow-and-black striped moth gives out the false unformation that it could strike back and maybe sting to the death if an enemy attacked it.

The world of insects is highly populated with great pretenders. Among the first to notice this was the 19th-century English naturalist H.W. Bates, who drew attention to the fact that some perfectly harmless insects frequently turn mimic to deceive potential enemies. A hornet moth, for instance, will try to pass itself off as a stinging hornet wasp in a form of behavior now known as Batesian mimicry, after its discoverer.

GETTING INTO SHAPE

Leaf insects are also mimics. While at rest during the day, they are almost invisible among the foliage on which they feed at night. However, their skills do not stop at that. If they had a regular exoskeleton, they would stand out from the nibbled leaves around them. To prevent this, they have developed a row of flanges that runs right around their abdomen. Other leaf insects cooperate by nibbling at them to make them even more leaflike. Their eggs are excellent mimics, too, and even experts find it hard to tell them apart from caterpillar droppings.

Some moths look like bundles of withered leaves; others resemble tangled foliage. Playing possum, or pretending to be dead, is another strategy frequently employed by some beetles to stop predators. Their ability to remain absolutely still is remarkable.

EATING HABITS

Nectar-collector

The bumblebee in this photograph uses its long proboscis to collect nectar from flowers and becomes coated in pollen.

Chomp, chomp, chomp go the jaws of a large, hungry caterpillar. It has been eating almost non-stop for two weeks now; and even though as a result of this, it has grown to about one thousand times its original size, it still continues to feed. Like nearly all butterflies and moths, however, once it is mature, it will only drink and never feed on solids again.

Not only do most insects have specially adapted mouth and body parts so that they can feed easily on the sort of diet they require, most also have distinctive behavioral traits that help them track down food with ease. Some, of course, are carnivores and predatory. They may even be very particular about their menu, seeking out just one type of prey for themselves or their larvae. A great number, however, are strictly plant-eaters, but they too may be fussy about what they include in their diet and only interested in a single species of plant in certain instances. But some plants – among them a North American clover – have developed a way of fighting back. They produce a chemical that attracts a predator of the moth caterpillar that thrives on their leaves. The predatory wasp then paralyzes the caterpillar and lays its eggs in it. When they hatch, the wasp larvae feed on the caterpillar.

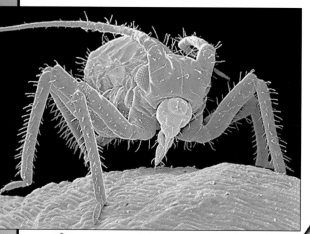

Thirsty pests

Aphids, like the one shown above under the microscope, are pests and feed by using their tubelike mouthparts to penetrate a leaf or stem. They do serious damage to a wide variety of plants.

Food exchange
The two ants shown here are passing food to each other. Many species of ant have developed a special section of the gut from which they can regurgitate food. They also give food to younger members of the colony, who in turn feed the queen and the larvae.

Always hungry
The desert locust that is framed by foliage in the photograph above is always hungry and was greedy even in its nymphal phase. As adults, they consume all sorts of plants from which they extract moisture. This is the only way they can survive in very hot and dry regions of the world, and is why they swarm and then devastate vegetation in such huge numbers.

Hungry caterpillars
It can be fun to watch a caterpillar reducing a leaf in size as it greedily eats its way along the edge. If there are many of them at large in a garden, however, several plants may be ruined. Caterpillars vary in their feeding habits. There are a number that make holes in leaves and some that only nibble at the undersides, leaving the upper surface and veins untouched. Sometimes, too, their feeding behavior alters with age as their mouthparts change.

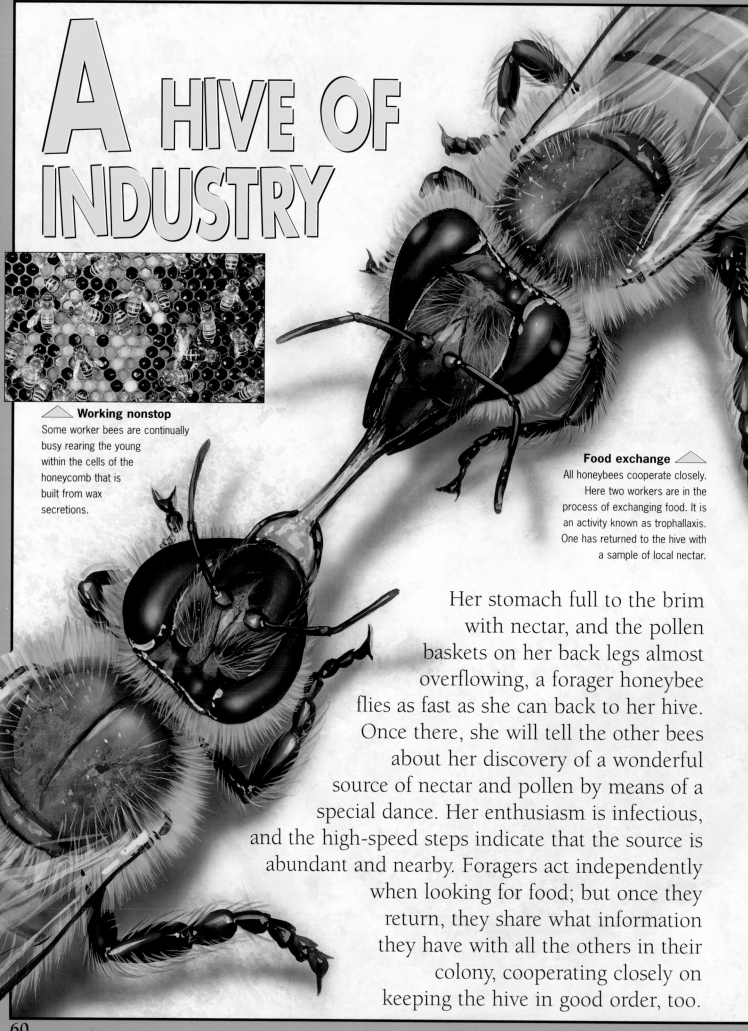

A HIVE OF INDUSTRY

Working nonstop
Some worker bees are continually busy rearing the young within the cells of the honeycomb that is built from wax secretions.

Food exchange
All honeybees cooperate closely. Here two workers are in the process of exchanging food. It is an activity known as trophallaxis. One has returned to the hive with a sample of local nectar.

Her stomach full to the brim with nectar, and the pollen baskets on her back legs almost overflowing, a forager honeybee flies as fast as she can back to her hive. Once there, she will tell the other bees about her discovery of a wonderful source of nectar and pollen by means of a special dance. Her enthusiasm is infectious, and the high-speed steps indicate that the source is abundant and nearby. Foragers act independently when looking for food; but once they return, they share what information they have with all the others in their colony, cooperating closely on keeping the hive in good order, too.

At first, the activity in a bee hive may appear quite disorderly. However, close examination reveals that every bee has its own specific tasks. Egg laying, for example, is the sole responsibility of the queen, and all the drones are expected to do is mate with her. The workers, meanwhile, are all female, and their particular duties vary a lot according to their age.

The workers are all sterile, which is just as well because they are kept busy enough maintaining the economy of the hive. There simply would not be enough time to breed.

HUGE NUMBERS

Wild honeybee colonies still exist, with nests built mainly in trees, but most honeybees now live in hives that are set up by beekeepers. At its height, a hive may contain up to as many as 60,000 workers, but the number of drones will be a small fraction of the female population. The drones live for only about one month and do not forage for their own food. The workers do this for them. The colony gets its revenge against these indolent males, however, when summer is over and the drones are thrown out by the workers.

Almost as soon as a worker is born, she has a job to do as a nurse for developing larvae. She is herself still fed by older workers but soon learns to take honey and pollen from the hive's stores. By the time she is two weeks old, she will be capable of building and repairing the hive's hexagonal cells and is now mature enough to leave the hive on short exploratory trips. Not yet ready to forage, she will nevertheless help store the pollen brought back by her older sisters. She is house-proud at an early stage, too, keeping the hive in good order and removing waste matter, as well as any bees that die in the hive.

These diligent workers fuss over the queen, too, licking and grooming her, and seeing that she is adequately fed. In return, she secretes a special food called the *queen substance*. All the workers share it, and pass it from one to another. Once three weeks old, she can join the foragers. Other newborn bees then take over her nursery duties.

Uncovered cells △
Within a hive and inside these hexagonal cells from which the wax caps have been removed to reveal their contents, you can see the white heads of developing honeybees at the prepupal stage. You should be able to identify their eyes and antennae in this photograph.

Protecting the comb
The worker bees below, all females, cooperate in many ways. Here they have settled into position close together in rows so they can protect the honeycomb in their hive from too much moisture. They may get damp themselves, but protection of the comb is more important to them.

Laden with pollen △
One of the two honeybees in the photograph above is heavily laden with pollen that it will store in the cells on which they are resting. These workers are tireless collectors, and there may be as many as 60,000 of them in a single hive. Only when it gets dark do they rest.

Live-in larder
A fly will lay her eggs on some steak if given the chance, so that when her larvae hatch, they will have a good source of food all around them on which to scavenge.

Foraging for food
These two worker wasps have found some fruit and are busy feeding on its flesh. They only feed in this way late in the season. Earlier in the year they feed on live insects and carrion.

A maggot's meal
Having emerged from the egg laid on some raw beef, this greenbottle maggot is busy feeding on it. It secretes special enzymes that liquefy this source of food so that it can easily be absorbed by its digestive system.

SCAVENGERS

Having waited until all was quiet and there was no one around, a cockroach has headed out in search of a meal. Tonight there is something sweet for its midnight snack. The aroma of the remains of a freshly baked cake, carelessly left uncovered, has reached it, and soon other cockroaches will come by, too, to enjoy some of this sugary feast.

Tempting crumbs
Try to clear away any leftovers after a meal, and keep the kitchen floor well swept and washed. In dirty surroundings cockroaches may emerge in large numbers, particularly if it is warm, and start to scavenge on the remains of your meals, spreading harmful bacteria as they go.

Scavenging might be considered an easy way to get a meal, whether it is one of meat or of plants. However, because leftovers or animal corpses can never be guaranteed, insects that have developed this type of feeding behavior must either be very active and prepared to travel considerable distances in search of sustenance or be able to digest a whole variety of foods.

WASTE DISPOSAL

Insects that scavenge also have an important part to play in the ecosystem by breaking down the fabric of their easy pickings as they feed on the bodies of dead creatures and the waste products of others. That is in fact why we see so few dead birds, mice, or squirrels even in the countryside. Insects will have helped with their disposal by scavenging on them.

Some carnivorous insects will take back pieces of flesh to their colonies so that others can bury them to ensure a supply of food for the next generation. Male scorpionflies, however, are among those that scavenge for another purpose. Not only do they feed off dead creatures themselves, they will also sometimes offer a meal to a female as a gift before mating. They have even been seen stealing an insect trapped in a spider's web in the attempt to woo a mate with this tasty morsel.

Snake snack

In the photograph above, hundreds of driver ants are making the most of their find and have begun to feed on a dead cobra. If you or any other animals disturb them when they are eating, the soldiers among them would approach and try to sting. They do not like being interrupted while they are scavenging on such a rich food source.

Time to take off

Within the swarm of honeybees on the branch of a sycamore tree the queen is protected by her workers. In early summer she leaves with an advance guard to look for a new nesting site in which to settle with about half the old hive's population.

Flying force

On hot days swarms of bluebottles may gather. Domestic pests that spread germs, they are seen here on the surface of a glass plate. Never eat anything from a surface on which they have crawled without washing it first.

SWARMING

Now that she has wriggled her way up through the sandy soil, a hatchling locust breaks the surface, and her soft body starts to harden. All around her other nymphs are beginning to hop around so that she feels compelled to hop, too. Soon a huge band of them will form, and before long the swarm will have eaten all the plants in its path. The area will finally be left entirely without any traces of greenery.

Milling around

Honeybees swarm on bright days and usually at around noon. When the nest or hive has become too crowded, the queen leaves to make room for a successor and a new generation of bees.

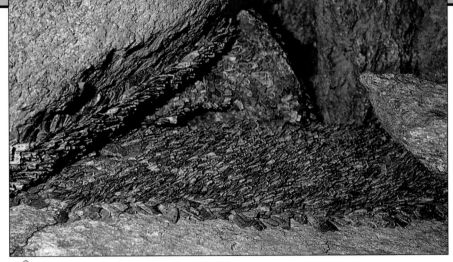

Masses of moths

In Australia a swarm of bogong moths rests together in their summer "camp" among granite boulders after their long annual migration.

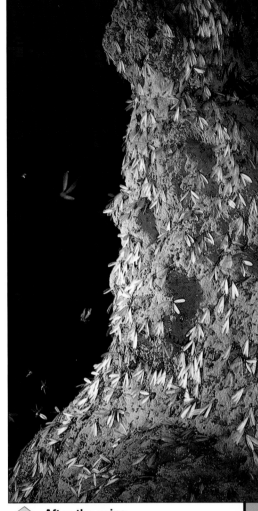

After the rains

Termites usually begin their nuptial flights shortly after heavy rains. You can see them in the photograph above, as they start to emerge from their mound.

For some insects swarming is a regular part of their annual lifecycle, ensuring that males and females are active at the same time, so that the chances of successful mating are all the higher. Usually this will involve spectacular numbers of insects all suddenly appearing over just a few days before, just as speedily, they disperse once more. Other insects swarm when conditions become overcrowded – if a mild winter has allowed more hibernating insects to survive than would normally be the case, for instance. Bees, too, will swarm when the hive's population becomes too great. Scouts sent out to find a suitable new home will soon return to communicate the whereabouts of an alternative home by means of a special dance. The swarm will then find its way there and move in. Unexpected rainfall may also create a sudden flourishing of plants, in turn causing a dramatic increase in the number of insects coming together to feed on them. Swarms such as these make a dazzling sight; but if the insects in them sting, be sure to avoid their path.

The devastators

Locusts, like those below, form enormous swarms and can devastate acres of land in only a few hours. They are even mentioned in the Old Testament as one of the ten plagues.

WHEN WINTER COMES

In search of warmer temperatures, every year millions of monarch butterflies instinctively travel about two thousand miles from Canada to Mexico before the harsh winters of the north so they will not freeze to death. The long return journey will start next spring.

A cozy corner
Nestling in the corner of a picture frame, a lacewing has settled in for the winter – an uninvited guest in this apartment, but one that will do no harm.

The journey south
Monarch butterflies somehow know that they must fly a long way south before winter comes. The next generation's return the following year is instinctive, too.

The long sleep
This hibernating queen wasp will spend the coldest months in a characteristic rigid position in a secret hiding place before waking up during the first warm, sunny days of spring. She will then start to look for nectar and build a nest.

Insects are not usually very good at generating their own heat and so cannot cope with cold weather. However, some have found ways around this problem. They will spend the coldest months of the year either at the egg stage or as pupae and at this time may be buried under the ground, where they are well insulated from frost or snow.

Some, such as the monarch butterflies, will migrate; and others, like ladybugs, will crowd together in large groups to keep warm, in a form of behavior known as *aggregation*. Those on the outside of these clumps might all perish in the cold, but those not exposed will probably survive.

COMING INDOORS

Look for insects in your home, too, during the coldest months of the year. Some will invade a warm house in the search for a winter retreat and could be lurking silently in a corner, where they hope to remain undisturbed until a change of season. You might perhaps find a queen wasp lying dormant. She will survive the winter; but the workers and males usually die off.

Huddling together
Ladybugs manage to survive in bad weather by huddling together in a cluster for warmth. You will sometimes find them on bark, in a porch, or even indoors.

HIDE-AND-SEEK

Perfectly still
Stick insects remain still by day, almost as if they are challenging predators to spot them among the vegetation that they so closely resemble.

So effective is its camouflage and so still its pose that, for a long while, the stick insect that has been resting on a branch has been undetected. One slight move, however, and a passing chameleon spots its next meal. The lizard's sticky tongue shoots out with lightning speed, and in a flash the helpless living twig meets an untimely end as it is gulped down greedily.

Clever camouflage
A keen-eyed photographer was lucky to spot this imperial moth in the Costa Rican jungle.

Hardly visible
You might think that this "prominent" moth in no way deserves such a name! It is almost invisible because its markings are so barklike. But its caterpillar is brightly colored, which is how it gets its name.

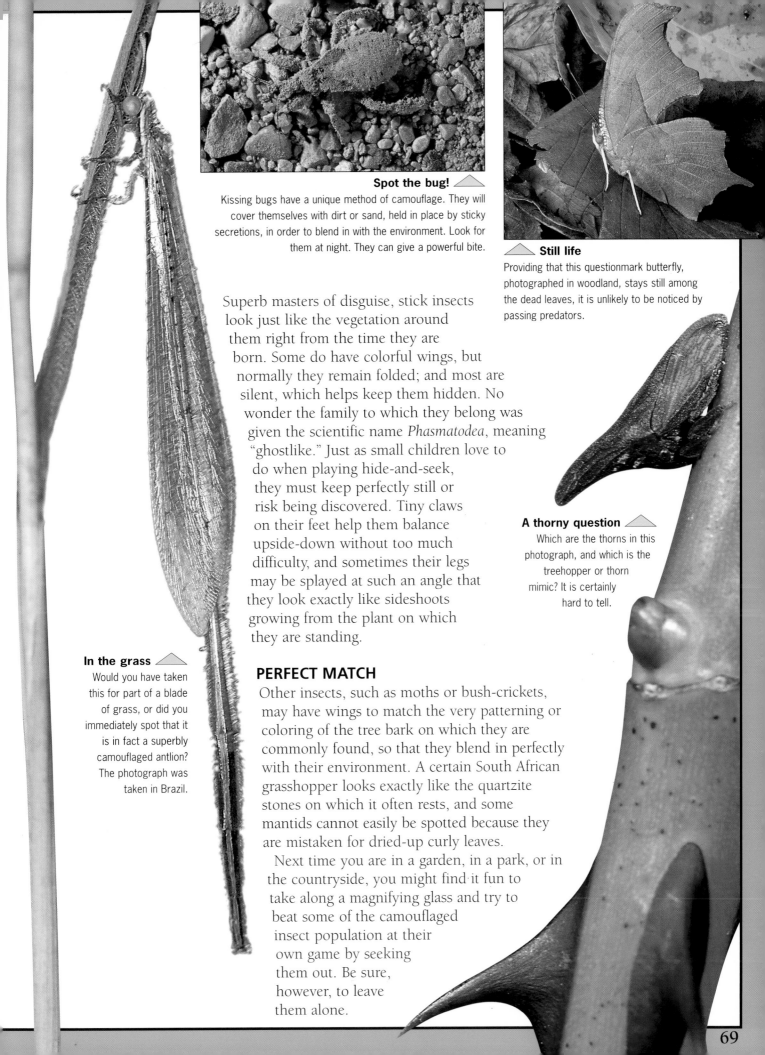

Kissing bugs have a unique method of camouflage. They will cover themselves with dirt or sand, held in place by sticky secretions, in order to blend in with the environment. Look for them at night. They can give a powerful bite.

Still life

Providing that this questionmark butterfly, photographed in woodland, stays still among the dead leaves, it is unlikely to be noticed by passing predators.

Superb masters of disguise, stick insects look just like the vegetation around them right from the time they are born. Some do have colorful wings, but normally they remain folded; and most are silent, which helps keep them hidden. No wonder the family to which they belong was given the scientific name *Phasmatodea*, meaning "ghostlike." Just as small children love to do when playing hide-and-seek, they must keep perfectly still or risk being discovered. Tiny claws on their feet help them balance upside-down without too much difficulty, and sometimes their legs may be splayed at such an angle that they look exactly like sideshoots growing from the plant on which they are standing.

A thorny question

Which are the thorns in this photograph, and which is the treehopper or thorn mimic? It is certainly hard to tell.

In the grass

Would you have taken this for part of a blade of grass, or did you immediately spot that it is in fact a superbly camouflaged antlion? The photograph was taken in Brazil.

PERFECT MATCH

Other insects, such as moths or bush-crickets, may have wings to match the very patterning or coloring of the tree bark on which they are commonly found, so that they blend in perfectly with their environment. A certain South African grasshopper looks exactly like the quartzite stones on which it often rests, and some mantids cannot easily be spotted because they are mistaken for dried-up curly leaves.

Next time you are in a garden, in a park, or in the countryside, you might find it fun to take along a magnifying glass and try to beat some of the camouflaged insect population at their own game by seeking them out. Be sure, however, to leave them alone.

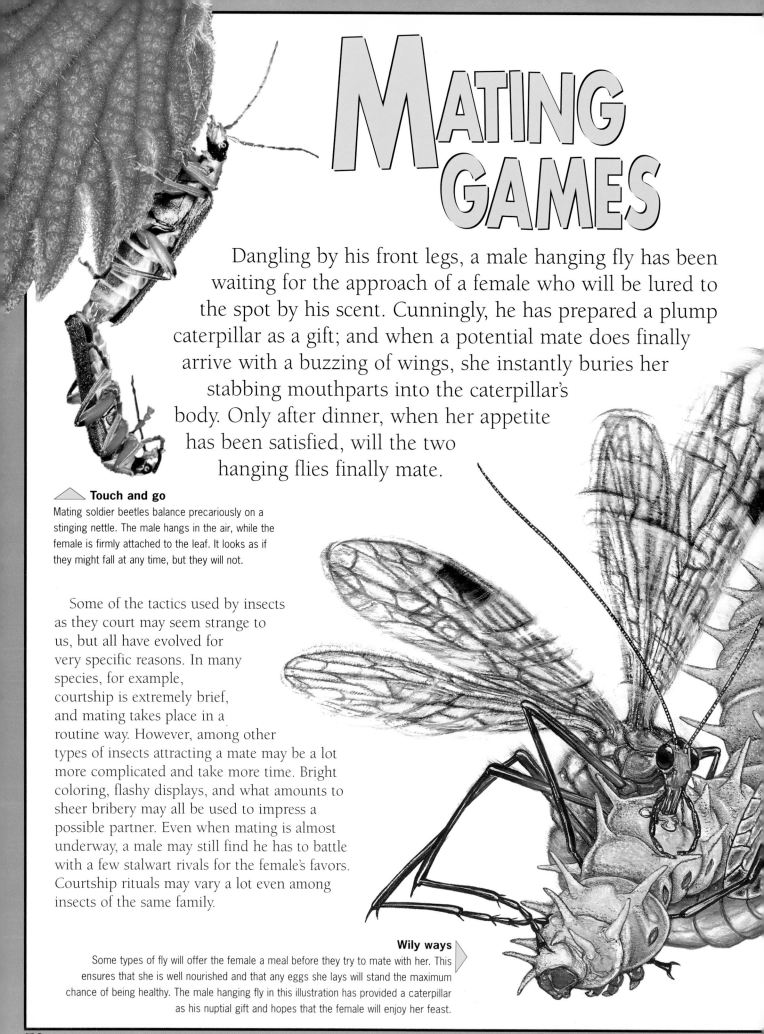

MATING GAMES

Dangling by his front legs, a male hanging fly has been waiting for the approach of a female who will be lured to the spot by his scent. Cunningly, he has prepared a plump caterpillar as a gift; and when a potential mate does finally arrive with a buzzing of wings, she instantly buries her stabbing mouthparts into the caterpillar's body. Only after dinner, when her appetite has been satisfied, will the two hanging flies finally mate.

△ Touch and go

Mating soldier beetles balance precariously on a stinging nettle. The male hangs in the air, while the female is firmly attached to the leaf. It looks as if they might fall at any time, but they will not.

Some of the tactics used by insects as they court may seem strange to us, but all have evolved for very specific reasons. In many species, for example, courtship is extremely brief, and mating takes place in a routine way. However, among other types of insects attracting a mate may be a lot more complicated and take more time. Bright coloring, flashy displays, and what amounts to sheer bribery may all be used to impress a possible partner. Even when mating is almost underway, a male may still find he has to battle with a few stalwart rivals for the female's favors. Courtship rituals may vary a lot even among insects of the same family.

Wily ways ▷

Some types of fly will offer the female a meal before they try to mate with her. This ensures that she is well nourished and that any eggs she lays will stand the maximum chance of being healthy. The male hanging fly in this illustration has provided a caterpillar as his nuptial gift and hopes that the female will enjoy her feast.

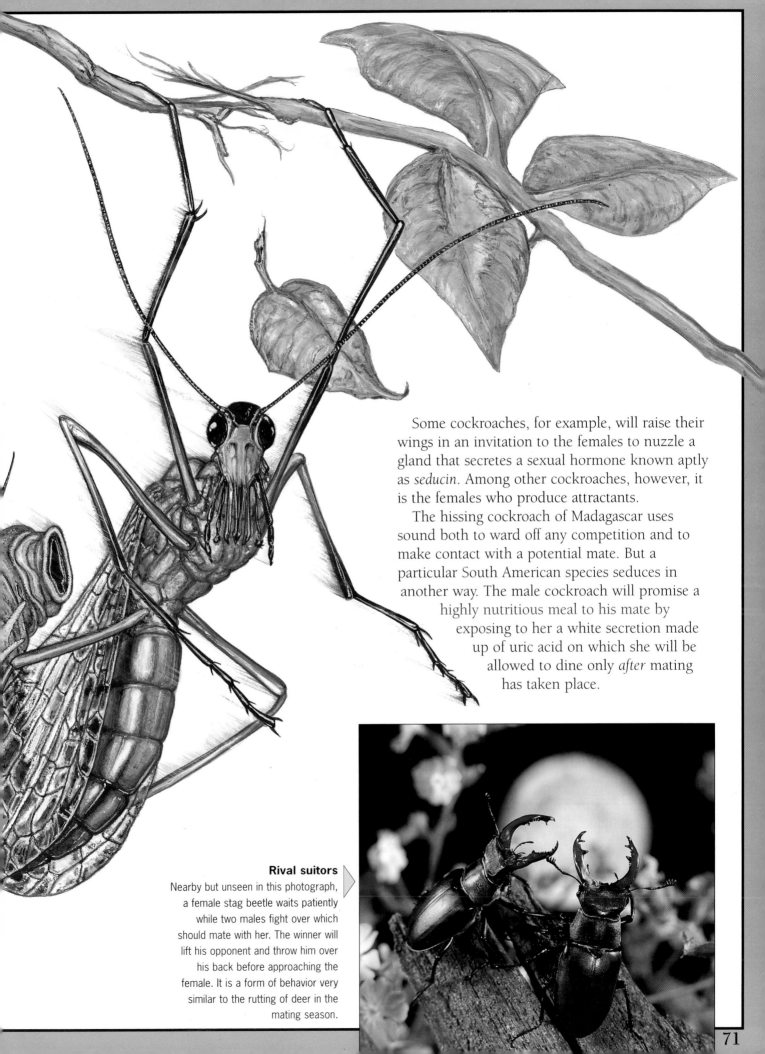

Some cockroaches, for example, will raise their wings in an invitation to the females to nuzzle a gland that secretes a sexual hormone known aptly as *seducin*. Among other cockroaches, however, it is the females who produce attractants.

The hissing cockroach of Madagascar uses sound both to ward off any competition and to make contact with a potential mate. But a particular South American species seduces in another way. The male cockroach will promise a highly nutritious meal to his mate by exposing to her a white secretion made up of uric acid on which she will be allowed to dine only *after* mating has taken place.

Rival suitors

Nearby but unseen in this photograph, a female stag beetle waits patiently while two males fight over which should mate with her. The winner will lift his opponent and throw him over his back before approaching the female. It is a form of behavior very similar to the rutting of deer in the mating season.

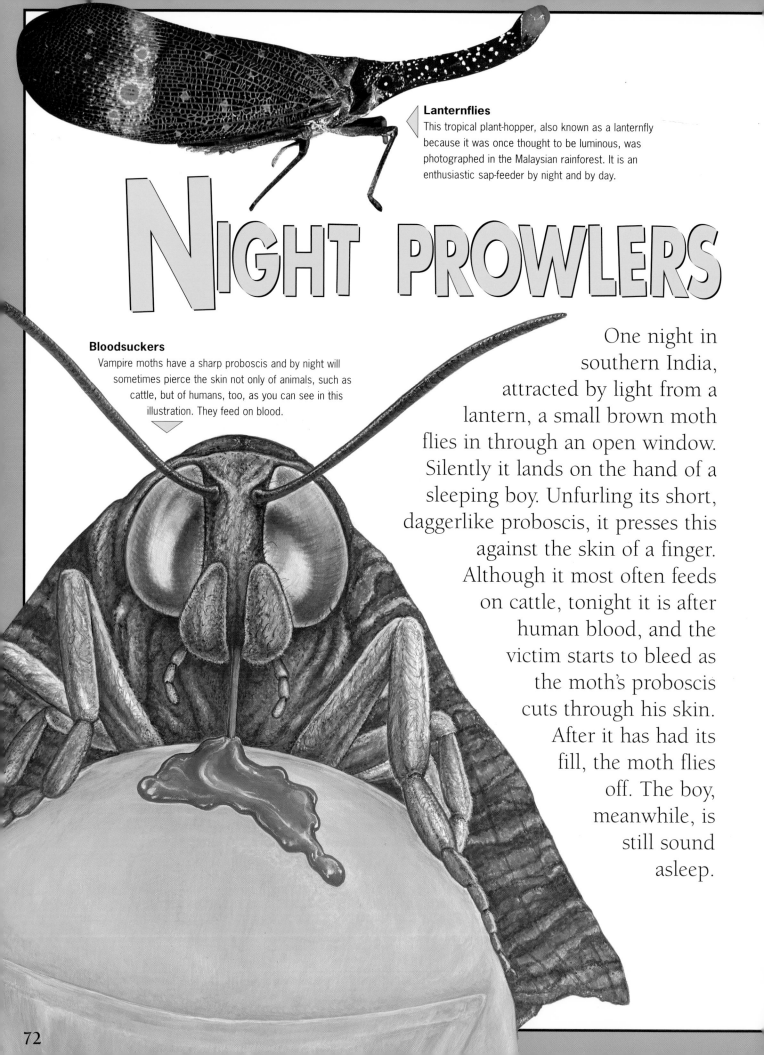

Lanternflies

This tropical plant-hopper, also known as a lanternfly because it was once thought to be luminous, was photographed in the Malaysian rainforest. It is an enthusiastic sap-feeder by night and by day.

NIGHT PROWLERS

Bloodsuckers

Vampire moths have a sharp proboscis and by night will sometimes pierce the skin not only of animals, such as cattle, but of humans, too, as you can see in this illustration. They feed on blood.

One night in southern India, attracted by light from a lantern, a small brown moth flies in through an open window. Silently it lands on the hand of a sleeping boy. Unfurling its short, daggerlike proboscis, it presses this against the skin of a finger. Although it most often feeds on cattle, tonight it is after human blood, and the victim starts to bleed as the moth's proboscis cuts through his skin. After it has had its fill, the moth flies off. The boy, meanwhile, is still sound asleep.

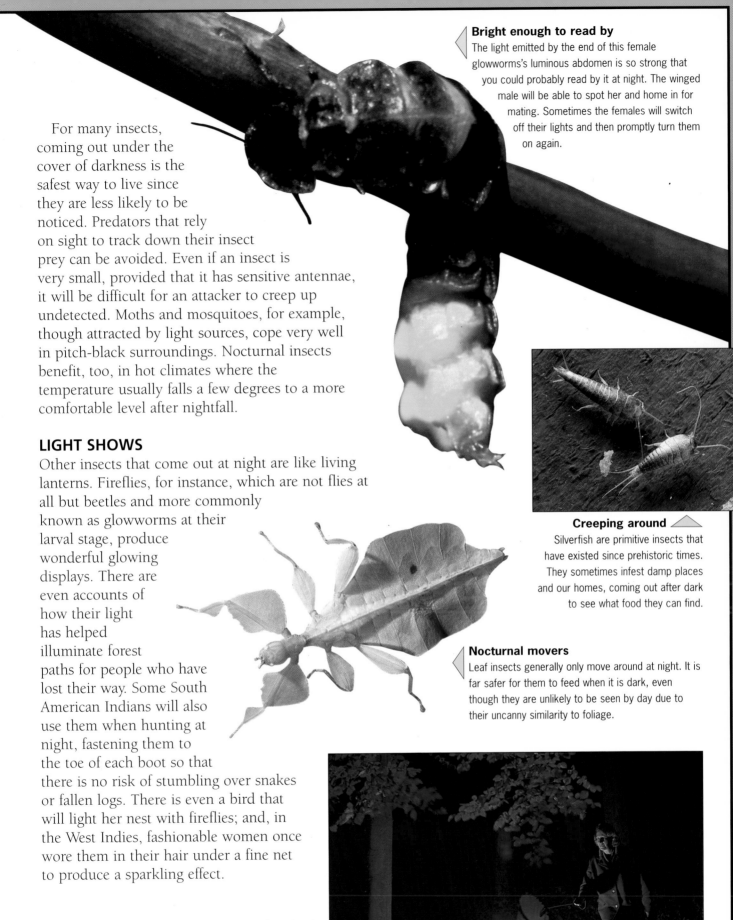

For many insects, coming out under the cover of darkness is the safest way to live since they are less likely to be noticed. Predators that rely on sight to track down their insect prey can be avoided. Even if an insect is very small, provided that it has sensitive antennae, it will be difficult for an attacker to creep up undetected. Moths and mosquitoes, for example, though attracted by light sources, cope very well in pitch-black surroundings. Nocturnal insects benefit, too, in hot climates where the temperature usually falls a few degrees to a more comfortable level after nightfall.

LIGHT SHOWS

Other insects that come out at night are like living lanterns. Fireflies, for instance, which are not flies at all but beetles and more commonly known as glowworms at their larval stage, produce wonderful glowing displays. There are even accounts of how their light has helped illuminate forest paths for people who have lost their way. Some South American Indians will also use them when hunting at night, fastening them to the toe of each boot so that there is no risk of stumbling over snakes or fallen logs. There is even a bird that will light her nest with fireflies; and, in the West Indies, fashionable women once wore them in their hair under a fine net to produce a sparkling effect.

Bright enough to read by
The light emitted by the end of this female glowworms's luminous abdomen is so strong that you could probably read by it at night. The winged male will be able to spot her and home in for mating. Sometimes the females will switch off their lights and then promptly turn them on again.

Creeping around
Silverfish are primitive insects that have existed since prehistoric times. They sometimes infest damp places and our homes, coming out after dark to see what food they can find.

Nocturnal movers
Leaf insects generally only move around at night. It is far safer for them to feed when it is dark, even though they are unlikely to be seen by day due to their uncanny similarity to foliage.

Moth-hunting
Moths are out and about at night. Entomologists, like the one in this photograph, who want to catch them therefore go out with special ultraviolet traps to which unwary moths will be attracted. With a little patience, this moth-hunter should find a few different specimens.

ON THE MOVE

Winter migration ▲

When the chilly days of autumn arrive, instead of hibernating, millions of monarch butterflies set off in a southerly direction from Canada to sunnier regions, such as Florida or Mexico.

Being able to get around is vital for most living creatures. They need to feed, find a mate, colonize new areas, perhaps, and escape from predators. However, no group of animals has found as many different ways of achieving such aims as the insects. Whether they jump, wriggle, walk, fly, hop, skate, or use jet propulsion, most insects will have perfected some form of motion and will always use it to their advantage. However, a number are extremely crafty and do not bother to expend any energy at all when getting from place to place. They simply hitch a ride. Others will hardly move at all once they are mature.

On the march ▲

Some ants march for most of the time in long columns and form killer armies, moving at a remarkable rate for their size. Soldier army ants, like the one above, guard them as they go.

But how do flying insects launch themselves into the air? Is it true that some march in huge armies? And why do a few migrate long distances? You are bound to be amazed by the very versatile movers of the insect kingdom.

◄ **On the hop**

Which insects excel at hopping? Fleas can jump to great heights, but there are other insects, too, that leap, as you will discover if you take a look at pages 82-83.

Speedy species ►

When making a dash for their prey, tiger beetles, avid predators, will scoot along at a fantastic rate, as shown in the photograph, right.

LIFTOFF!

On a moonlit night in the middle of summer two earwigs crawl slowly to the top of a large yellow flower. With great care one of them now lifts his wing cases and starts to unfold his wings. Once they are fully spread, he then takes a leap from the plant and is in the air after a few preparatory flaps. The female – smaller and with a simple pincer structure at the end of the abdomen – will follow him shortly.

Unfolding his wings
The male earwig, left, has already opened his wings. When not in use, however, they are kept folded like a very complicated piece of origami.

Jumping up
Once they are in the air, hoverflies will be true to their name and hover for most of the time, beating their wings at a phenomenal 1,000 times per second. They can take off quickly, too, as in the multiple exposure shown here.

A flying leap

This ichneumon fly – not a true fly but in the same order as wasps – has just taken off from a dead branch. Its flight looks particularly graceful because of its long body. It is parasitic and probably looking for a host on which to lay its eggs.

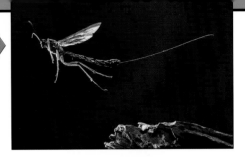

▲ **Away we go!**
In this multiflash image taken at night, you can see three stages of takeoff as an iron prominent moth from Europe launches itself from a leaf.

All species of earwigs with large, delicate hindwings always keep them folded under their *tegmina*, or wing cases, when at rest. The process of folding and unfolding them is extremely complicated. There may even be as many as 40 layers of wing. (If you take a piece of paper that is the same size as this page and try to fold it 40 times, you will see how difficult it is to do this. An earwig's wings are minute in comparison and so much harder to fold.)

ACHIEVING FLIGHT

We know from fossil evidence that winged insects have existed for over 300 million years. Possibly, paleontologists have suggested, wings first developed among aquatic insects that had paddles for getting around in and on the water. These "paddles" may have become larger and more powerful with time, so that speed increased dramatically. These organs then became more like wings, and liftoff was a further natural development.

Only adult insects have fully developed and functional wings, although they can sometimes be seen as wing buds in an insect nymph. To achieve liftoff, an insect has to overcome both gravity and resistance to movement. It will use its legs to spring into the air and then activates its flight muscles.

▲ **Open cases**
The front wings of beetles have evolved into hard cases known as elytra. They protect the more delicate hindwings when the insect is not using them. The elytra still have a function, however, providing lift as they open so that the beetle can take to the air.

◄ **Overcoming gravity**
When a cardinal beetle takes to the air, it first takes a little hop. At the same time, its nervous system makes the bright wing cases open. It is soon overcoming gravity.

ACROBATICS

▲ **Topsy-turvy**

Flies are not only so speedy that they are almost impossible to catch, they can even land the wrong way up so that their feet seem to dangle from the roof. It is a landing position that does not bother them at all.

Have you ever watched flies do a half-spin, land, and then walk upside down on the ceiling, just as the fantasy character Spiderman might do? Flies can perform in this way without slipping or stumbling at all and may remain the wrong way up for quite some time before taking to the air again. They can climb up and down walls, too, without any difficulty. Thanks to the sticky pads on the soles of their feet, they have a firm grip on both horizontal and vertical surfaces. What superb acrobats flies are!

Hovering on the spot and moving backward in the air can also be counted among a fly's talents. Its *halteres*, or modified hindwings, are used to stabilize the insect in flight. They are particularly helpful when it comes to performing what to us seem to be amazing tricks. Dragonflies can also go backward and may turn somersaults in the air at times. In fact, it is their flying speed and agility that help them both catch a meal and escape many predators that might otherwise only too easily make a meal of them.

TWIST AND SHOUT

Other insects are superb acrobats, too, and in several cases their antics are again vital to survival. If they happen to fall upside down on their backs, click beetles, for example, can throw themselves up to one foot in the air and straighten their stance so that they land the right way up once more, to the accompaniment of a loud clicking sound. Mating, meanwhile, may require considerable acrobatic activity for a number of insects and in a few species may even take place on the wing.

◀ **Taking the plunge**

This mantis nymph is not yet mature; but even at this early stage falling from one surface to another does not present any difficulties. Its wings have not yet formed, otherwise it might have used them to ensure a safe landing.

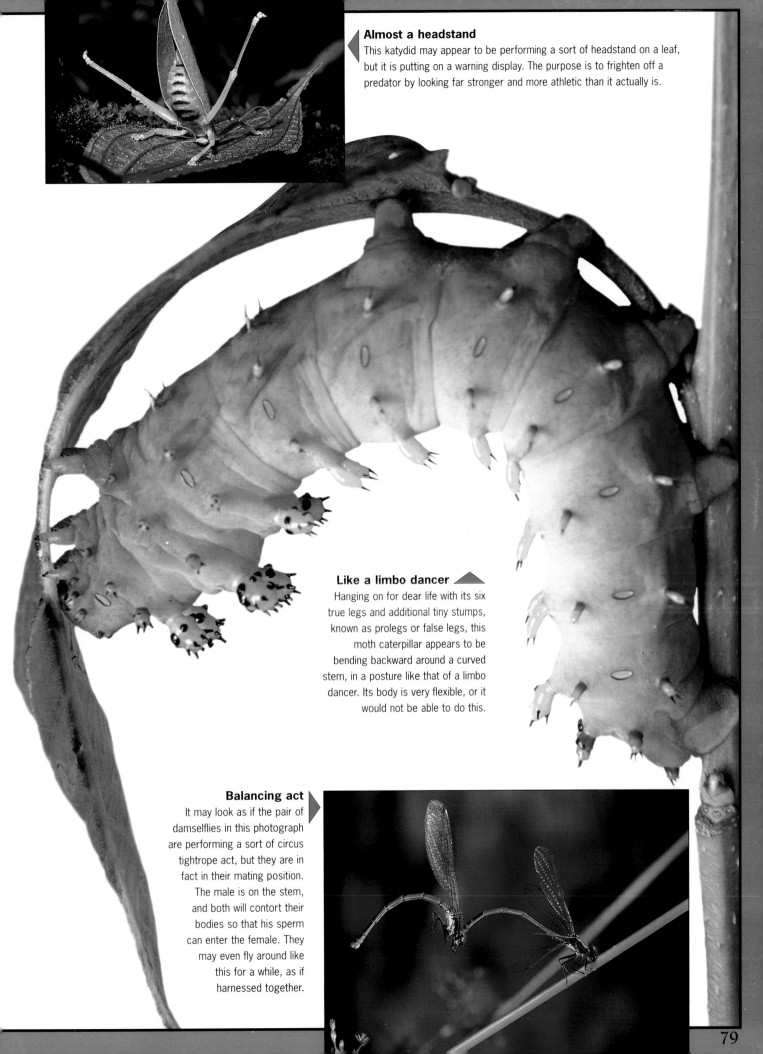

Almost a headstand

This katydid may appear to be performing a sort of headstand on a leaf, but it is putting on a warning display. The purpose is to frighten off a predator by looking far stronger and more athletic than it actually is.

Like a limbo dancer

Hanging on for dear life with its six true legs and additional tiny stumps, known as prolegs or false legs, this moth caterpillar appears to be bending backward around a curved stem, in a posture like that of a limbo dancer. Its body is very flexible, or it would not be able to do this.

Balancing act

It may look as if the pair of damselflies in this photograph are performing a sort of circus tightrope act, but they are in fact in their mating position. The male is on the stem, and both will contort their bodies so that his sperm can enter the female. They may even fly around like this for a while, as if harnessed together.

▲ Lively larvae
Seen dangling from
pondweed, this dragonfly
larva spends around four years
underwater before reaching
adulthood. It excels as an
aquatic predator.

In the water
Midges (tiny flies) do not enter the
water as adults, but their larvae,
shown below, creep into fast
streams. They have gills to help
them breathe underwater. At the
end of the pupal stage they float
to the surface and break out of
the pupae to fly away.
▼

GREAT SWIMMERS

Hanging motionless just below the
water's surface, a predatory diving
beetle waits patiently. As soon as it
spies a smaller insect that it fancies
for its lunch, however, two oarlike
back legs spring out from the sides
of its smooth, shiny body, and
with a couple of thrusts the
beetle starts to hurtle through
the water at a tremendous rate.
It will soon catch its prey.

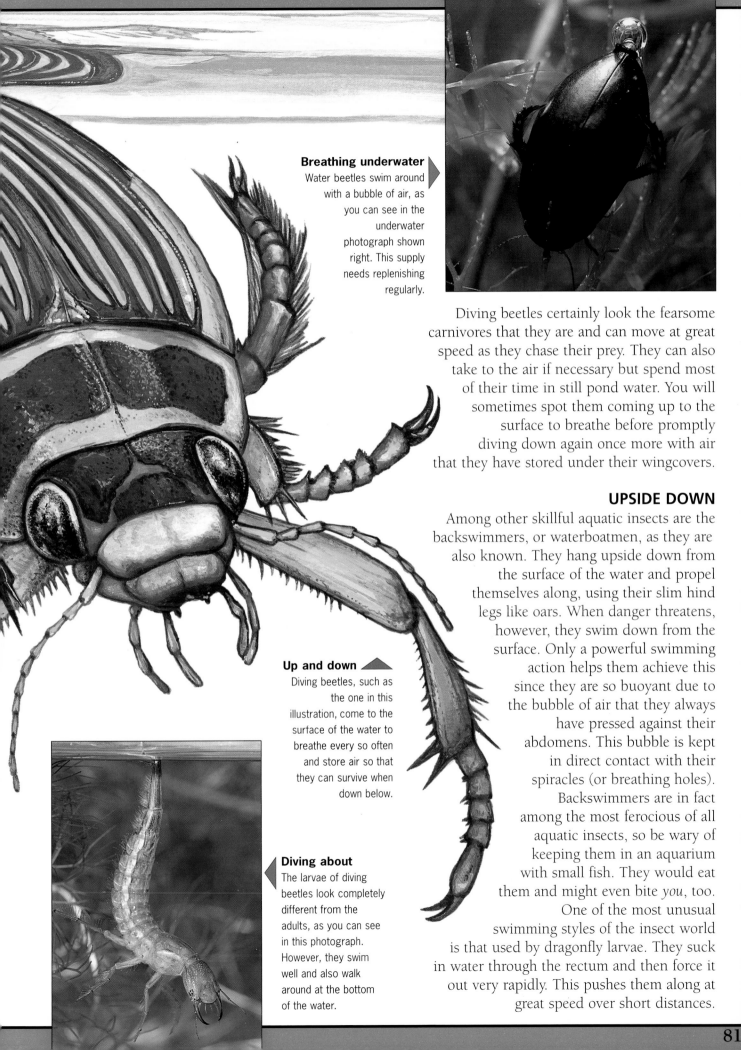

Breathing underwater
Water beetles swim around with a bubble of air, as you can see in the underwater photograph shown right. This supply needs replenishing regularly.

Diving beetles certainly look the fearsome carnivores that they are and can move at great speed as they chase their prey. They can also take to the air if necessary but spend most of their time in still pond water. You will sometimes spot them coming up to the surface to breathe before promptly diving down again once more with air that they have stored under their wingcovers.

UPSIDE DOWN

Among other skillful aquatic insects are the backswimmers, or waterboatmen, as they are also known. They hang upside down from the surface of the water and propel themselves along, using their slim hind legs like oars. When danger threatens, however, they swim down from the surface. Only a powerful swimming action helps them achieve this since they are so buoyant due to the bubble of air that they always have pressed against their abdomens. This bubble is kept in direct contact with their spiracles (or breathing holes). Backswimmers are in fact among the most ferocious of all aquatic insects, so be wary of keeping them in an aquarium with small fish. They would eat them and might even bite *you*, too.

One of the most unusual swimming styles of the insect world is that used by dragonfly larvae. They suck in water through the rectum and then force it out very rapidly. This pushes them along at great speed over short distances.

Up and down
Diving beetles, such as the one in this illustration, come to the surface of the water to breathe every so often and store air so that they can survive when down below.

Diving about
The larvae of diving beetles look completely different from the adults, as you can see in this photograph. However, they swim well and also walk around at the bottom of the water.

Froghoppers

These small insects are up to half an inch long and are named because of their froglike leaping on the plants and shrubs on which they feed. They closely resemble leafhoppers but have fewer spines on their hindlegs.

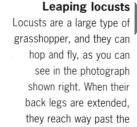

Leaping locusts

Locusts are a large type of grasshopper, and they can hop and fly, as you can see in the photograph shown right. When their back legs are extended, they reach way past the abdomen and help them take huge, bounding leaps.

Leafhoppers

As they hop from plant to plant, leafhoppers frequently spread plant diseases and are also serious crop pests. They are common jumping insects and look much like froghoppers, except that they have slimmer bodies.

ON THE HOP

As the weak spring sunlight warms the bark of a fallen tree, a chipmunk jumps down, and his movement disturbs the blanket covering of thousands of springtails. They leap away in panic; and even though they are tiny, the combined effect is bewildering to the chipmunk, who runs for cover. The force with which the springtails launch themselves takes them several times their own body length into the air.

Springing about

Even though it is under one-quarter of an inch long, a springtail still has remarkable control over its body movement. It has a special leaping organ known as a furcula at its rear. It is held underneath by a catch but released when the insect wants to hop, so that it is tossed into the air.

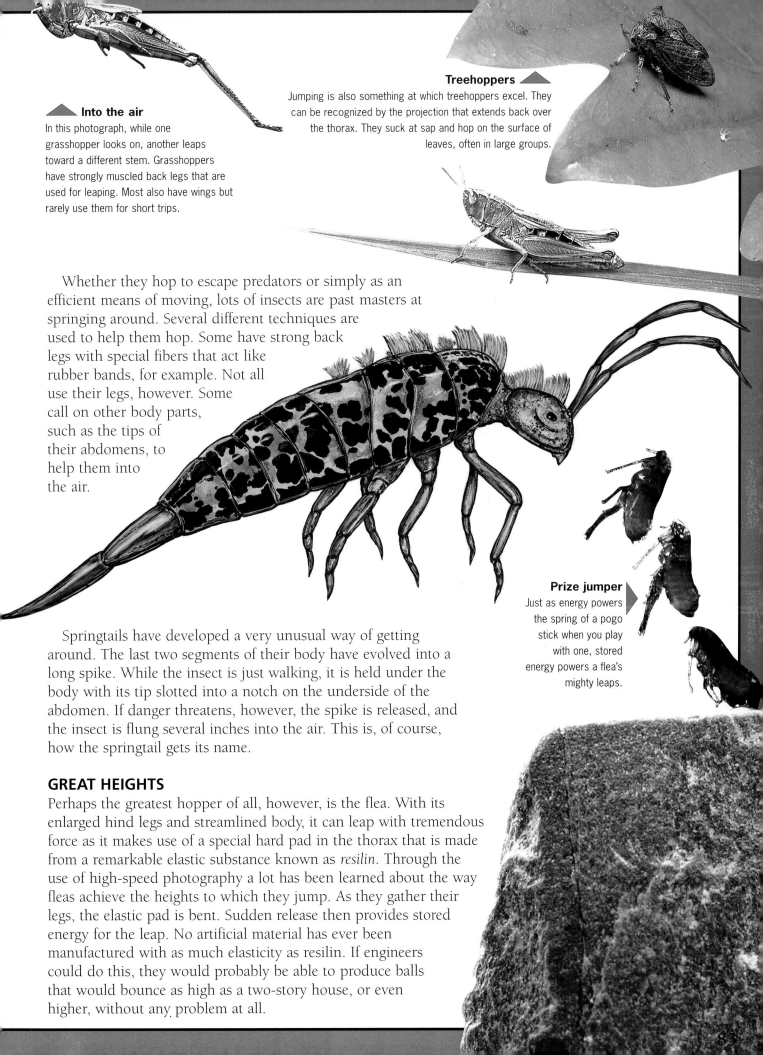

Into the air

In this photograph, while one grasshopper looks on, another leaps toward a different stem. Grasshoppers have strongly muscled back legs that are used for leaping. Most also have wings but rarely use them for short trips.

Treehoppers

Jumping is also something at which treehoppers excel. They can be recognized by the projection that extends back over the thorax. They suck at sap and hop on the surface of leaves, often in large groups.

Whether they hop to escape predators or simply as an efficient means of moving, lots of insects are past masters at springing around. Several different techniques are used to help them hop. Some have strong back legs with special fibers that act like rubber bands, for example. Not all use their legs, however. Some call on other body parts, such as the tips of their abdomens, to help them into the air.

Springtails have developed a very unusual way of getting around. The last two segments of their body have evolved into a long spike. While the insect is just walking, it is held under the body with its tip slotted into a notch on the underside of the abdomen. If danger threatens, however, the spike is released, and the insect is flung several inches into the air. This is, of course, how the springtail gets its name.

Prize jumper

Just as energy powers the spring of a pogo stick when you play with one, stored energy powers a flea's mighty leaps.

GREAT HEIGHTS

Perhaps the greatest hopper of all, however, is the flea. With its enlarged hind legs and streamlined body, it can leap with tremendous force as it makes use of a special hard pad in the thorax that is made from a remarkable elastic substance known as *resilin*. Through the use of high-speed photography a lot has been learned about the way fleas achieve the heights to which they jump. As they gather their legs, the elastic pad is bent. Sudden release then provides stored energy for the leap. No artificial material has ever been manufactured with as much elasticity as resilin. If engineers could do this, they would probably be able to produce balls that would bounce as high as a two-story house, or even higher, without any problem at all.

SKIMMING ALONG

Walking on water
The bodies of pond-skaters are covered with silver water-repellent hairs that prevent hem from becoming too damp. They frequently jump considerable distances but never break the water's surface. Their hind legs steer them along.

Two very long-legged pond-skaters appear to be resting on the still surface of a pond but are always at the ready. Suitable prey might chance to wander by, and if so, the two predators will pounce. If one type of rove beetle is in the vicinity, however, they may not be so lucky, and a deadly skating competition, with the loser ending up as lunch, might begin. This rove beetle has a remarkable method of moving. It can secrete a drop of fluid from the tip of its abdomen, and the fluid will lower the surface tension of the water behind it so that it is drawn forward at a rapid rate without much effort. This is a fantastic means of making a speedy get-away to safety or of accelerating in the role of predator.

Fast and furious
Pond-skaters are so quick on their feet as they skim the surface of the water that these carnivores can easily catch an unwary insect such as the bee in this photograph. It had only come to the pond for a drink but lost its life to the skater.

Darting around
This skimmer dragonfly, resting on a fragrant waterlily, is an excellent flier. As its name suggests, it particularly excels at skimming over water.

Treading the surface
Pond-skaters are so confident and stable on the surface of the water that they can even mate there, as shown in this photograph.

Insects weigh so little that they can frequently take advantage of the phenomenon of surface tension. Indeed, if they are light enough and can spread their weight, they are able, literally, to walk on water without going through the surface. Then, by using rowing motions with their legs, they can skate around on the surface at an impressive rate. If they are predatory, the surface of the water will also help them track down their prey. Any movement on the surface will make ripples travel outward. Then all the predatory insects have to do is home in on their prey. Backswimmers, meanwhile, skate upside down just below the surface of the water. This stance seems to be controlled by light. In fact, scientists have found that if these small but fierce carnivorous insects are placed in a tank lighted from below, they start to swim the right way up, not on their backs.

OVER THE OCEAN

Sea-skaters, meanwhile, though possibly hundreds of miles from the nearest land mass, move in the same way as pond-skaters but over the deep ocean surfaces. Some dragonflies will also skim along over ponds, pools, lakes, streams, or rivers before mating. The females will lay their eggs on reeds, in mud, or in the actual water.

Gyrating away
If disturbed, entire colonies of this species of yellow aphids will start to dance, twisting their bodies in the attempt to stop predators.

LET'S DANCE!

There is a lot of activity going on in the hive, and bees are busy exchanging information. A forager has recently returned to perform what is known as a round dance. The other bees appear fascinated by what she is doing. She has returned with some nectar and shares it while turning around in circles every few seconds as if the star act at a hive disco. Her dance is both energetic and noisy – sure signs that not only is the nectar of excellent quality, but that it is nearby. This is even more promising than yesterday, when another returned to perform a waggle dance, involving a figure-of-eight formation and much abdomen-shaking. That dance also provided information about a source of nectar, but the type of dance indicated the source to be further away.

When we dance, it is just a form of exercise or to show off. When bees start moving rhythmically, however, they have information to impart. Entomologists have proved this by marking a worker bee and giving it an artificial but rich food source. They then let it return to its home but prevented it from leaving the hive. Other workers from the same hive were nevertheless able to locate the food source, having obtained information as to its whereabouts from the imprisoned bee.

In another experiment almost all the workers who had made direct contact with a round-dancing messenger were able to find a new food source in under five minutes. Such *a round* dance indicates that flowers are fewer than 80 feet away, but a *waggle* dance performance announces that the food source may be as far as 300 feet from the hive.

The number of times the bee waggles its abdomen communicates the distance, and the angle at which the dance is performed signals the angle between the sun and the food supply. Scout bees also perform a special dance when they want to advise about a new nesting site. If there are several possible sites, they will dance at different angles for different lengths of time and at different speeds. It is as if they are discussing the suitability of each site. After more scouts have gone to assess the sites, they then indicate that a decision has been reached by performing the same dance routine. If, however, you see bees doing a sort of fan dance at the entrance to a hive, they are trying to cool it down.

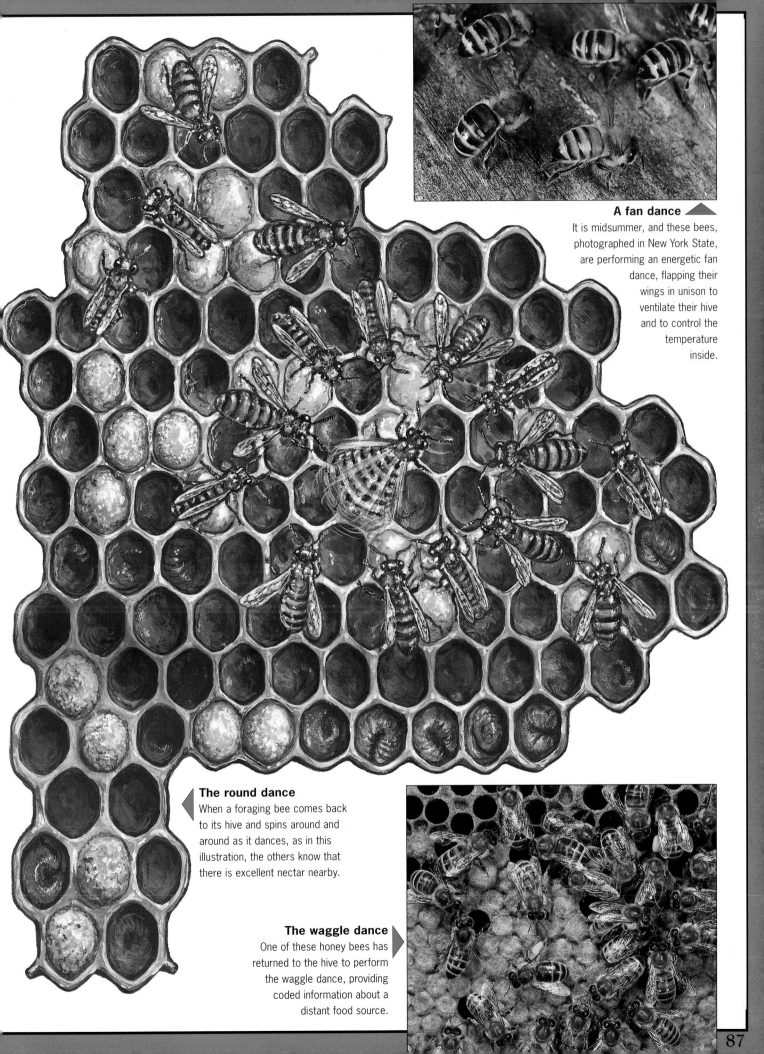

A fan dance ◄▲
It is midsummer, and these bees, photographed in New York State, are performing an energetic fan dance, flapping their wings in unison to ventilate their hive and to control the temperature inside.

The round dance
When a foraging bee comes back to its hive and spins around and around as it dances, as in this illustration, the others know that there is excellent nectar nearby.

The waggle dance ►
One of these honey bees has returned to the hive to perform the waggle dance, providing coded information about a distant food source.

HANGING AROUND

In midair

A hummingbird hawk moth can beat its wings at up to 300 times each second. This movement is so fast that it is almost invisible as the moth remains suspended in the air.

Hummingbird hawk moths, like the one shown *above*, spend most of their time traveling from flower to flower or simply resting. Every now and then, however, as they fly, they will suddenly stop in midair and start to hover. If the flower over which they are hovering produces the sort of nectar that they like, without landing they will uncurl their long proboscis and start to suck up the sweet substance. They do this frequently since they need to boost their energy levels for all that speedy hovering.

High-speed hover

Hoverflies, as their name suggests, can hang in the air by beating their wings at an extremely fast rate, just like other superb hoverers. To achieve this, contact between the nervous system and their muscles must be very finely tuned.

Just like a helicopter

If you have ever watched a helicopter hovering over a site before landing, you will recognize a similar whirring of wings when a hoverbee approaches a flower.

Among the most amazing sights in the whole of the insect kingdom is the hovering of the hummingbird hawk moths. When they stop dead-still in the air, it is almost as if they must be hanging from some sort of invisible thread. Dragonflies can do this, too. Being able to hover has a number of advantages. Nectar-feeders will be able to approach flowers on which it might otherwise be difficult to land, and predatory insects will be able to maintain suitable vantage points from which to watch for prey. With their keen eyesight, powerful jaws, and grasping legs, dragonflies are well adapted for hunting; and when they hover in midair, they will be able to dart after a victim at the very first sign of one.

Some insects have incorporated hovering into their courtship rituals. Only a very healthy insect can generate enough energy to hover. Healthy genes will then be passed on so that the next generation is likely to be healthy, too.

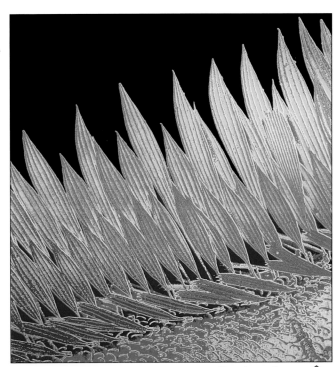

Beating wings

Among the most accomplished hoverers of all, mosquitoes beat their wings at a phenomenal rate. As they hover, the edges of their wings, shown above, pick up lots of information about environmental conditions.

Flower power

The nectar on which this soft-bodied, furry, beelike fly feeds provides the energy for it to hover over other flowers. Then, in turn, it will suck up more sweetness.

IMMIGRANTS

Biological control
The larvae in the photograph above bore holes into prickly pear cacti and were introduced to Australia to control these plants.

Out of Europe
German wasps like these were introduced from Europe and are now a terrible pest in Australia.

A family recently returned home from a vacation in the Canary Islands and brought back with them an exotic plant as a souvenir. Within a few days, however, scores of greedy termites had begun to emerge from the pot and started to colonize their house. Everything made of wood is now at risk from the greedy insects, particularly since they multiply so rapidly. These pests have even been known to bring whole buildings to the ground. As soon as they are discovered, it will be time to call in the pest controllers. Perhaps that wonderful plant was not such a good idea as a memento after all.

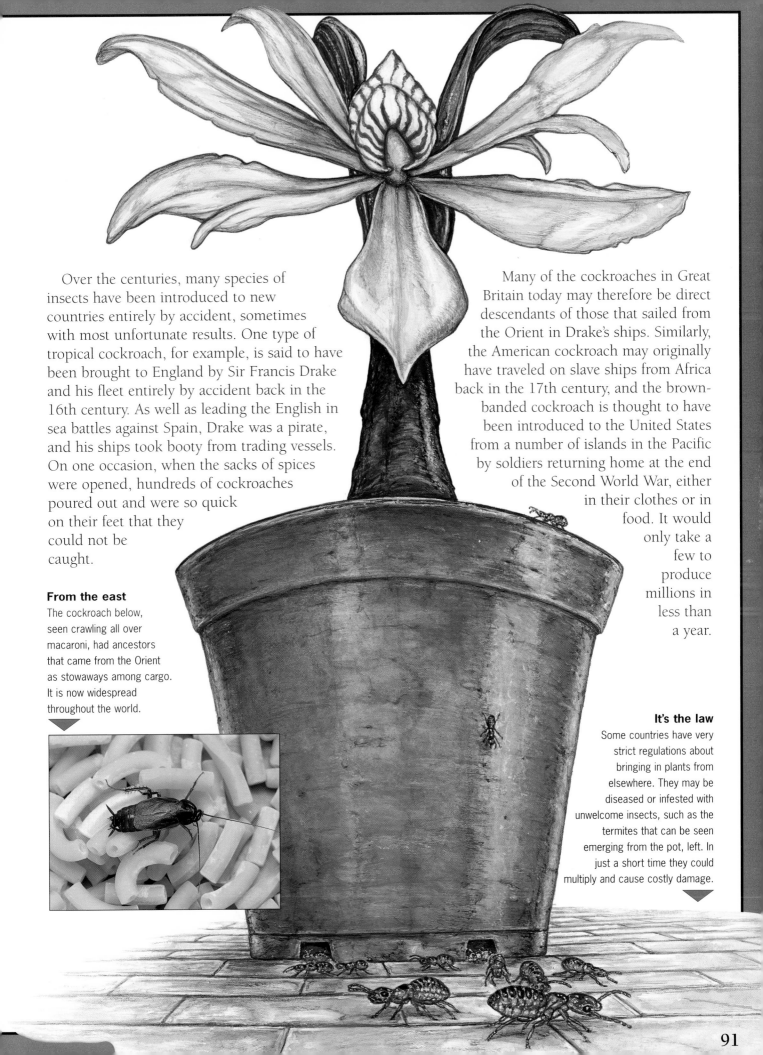

Over the centuries, many species of insects have been introduced to new countries entirely by accident, sometimes with most unfortunate results. One type of tropical cockroach, for example, is said to have been brought to England by Sir Francis Drake and his fleet entirely by accident back in the 16th century. As well as leading the English in sea battles against Spain, Drake was a pirate, and his ships took booty from trading vessels. On one occasion, when the sacks of spices were opened, hundreds of cockroaches poured out and were so quick on their feet that they could not be caught.

From the east

The cockroach below, seen crawling all over macaroni, had ancestors that came from the Orient as stowaways among cargo. It is now widespread throughout the world.

Many of the cockroaches in Great Britain today may therefore be direct descendants of those that sailed from the Orient in Drake's ships. Similarly, the American cockroach may originally have traveled on slave ships from Africa back in the 17th century, and the brown-banded cockroach is thought to have been introduced to the United States from a number of islands in the Pacific by soldiers returning home at the end of the Second World War, either in their clothes or in food. It would only take a few to produce millions in less than a year.

It's the law

Some countries have very strict regulations about bringing in plants from elsewhere. They may be diseased or infested with unwelcome insects, such as the termites that can be seen emerging from the pot, left. In just a short time they could multiply and cause costly damage.

MAKING TRACKS

Now that the heat of the midday sun has subsided a little, a leopard grasshopper wends its way across the sand, leaving behind it clear evidence that it has passed through this dry environment. The trail made by its six legs will, of course, be of interest to potential predators, for whom this insect will provide a tasty meal if it gets caught.

Trail-blazer
Just as we do if we walk on wet mud or on sand, insects will frequently leave tracks behind them as they walk. This highly enlarged illustration of a grasshopper and its trail shows the sort of marks that you may be able to spot. Hunting for insect tracks is not easy, which makes finding some all the more exciting.

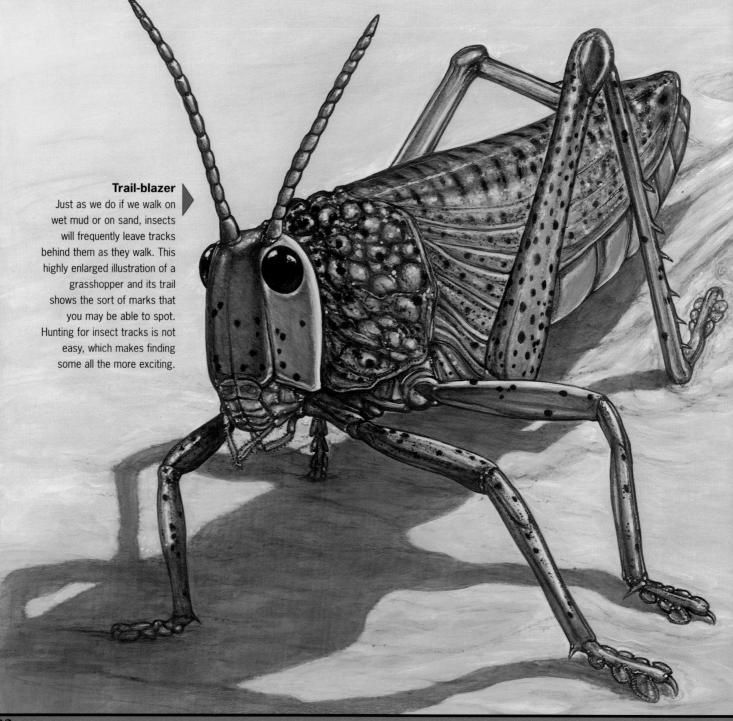

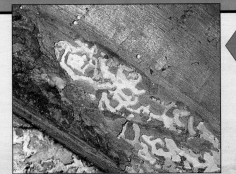

As the larva grows, the tracks that it makes in a leaf become progressively wider, too. Some larvae will feed in this way inside rushes or reeds, or in the stems of crops such as corn.

SECRET FEEDERS

Those insect larvae that feed within plant tissue and eat away at the internal layers of cells usually leave large areas of a plant looking blotchy or white if you hold it up to the light. Sometimes it can be completely see-through in places. While eating, the larvae will have taken in all the healthy green parts of the leaf within which they have been burrowing.

When insect larvae feed in this way, they will rarely be noticed by predators such as birds and so usually survive to adulthood. It is even possible to tell which type of caterpillar or other insect larva was in a leaf-tunnel by the shape of the tracks. All will leave the outside of a stalk or leaf undamaged, however.

If you ever spot holes in the surface of wooden beams or an item of furniture, it is a sure sign of woodworm invasion. Deep inside the timber, and therefore invisible to you, there will be a whole network of tracks that the larvae made as they worked their way along, feeding as they progressed.

Tracks can be left by insects not only on the ground but actually on the inside of leaves by the larvae of small moths or flies. These insects lay their eggs on the leaves; and when a larva hatches, it will bite its way into the leaf and then crawl and feed between the layers. Some of these leaf-miners burrow from the center outward, but others make tracks that wind without a set pattern, just like a meandering river all over the inside of a leaf.

Telltale signs
The galleries or tracks that you can see in the photograph of an apple tree leaf, below, have been made by a mining micromoth larva. The leaf has been severely damaged.

Minute miners
The meandering trails that are clearly visible inside the leaf, below, have been left by the greedy larvae of leaf-mining insects as they fed within it in the rainforests of Venezuela.

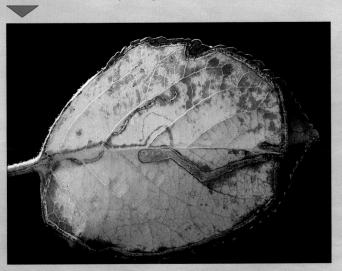

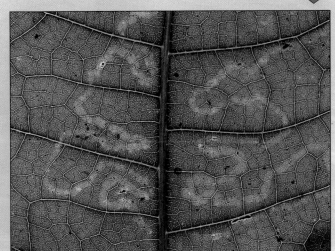

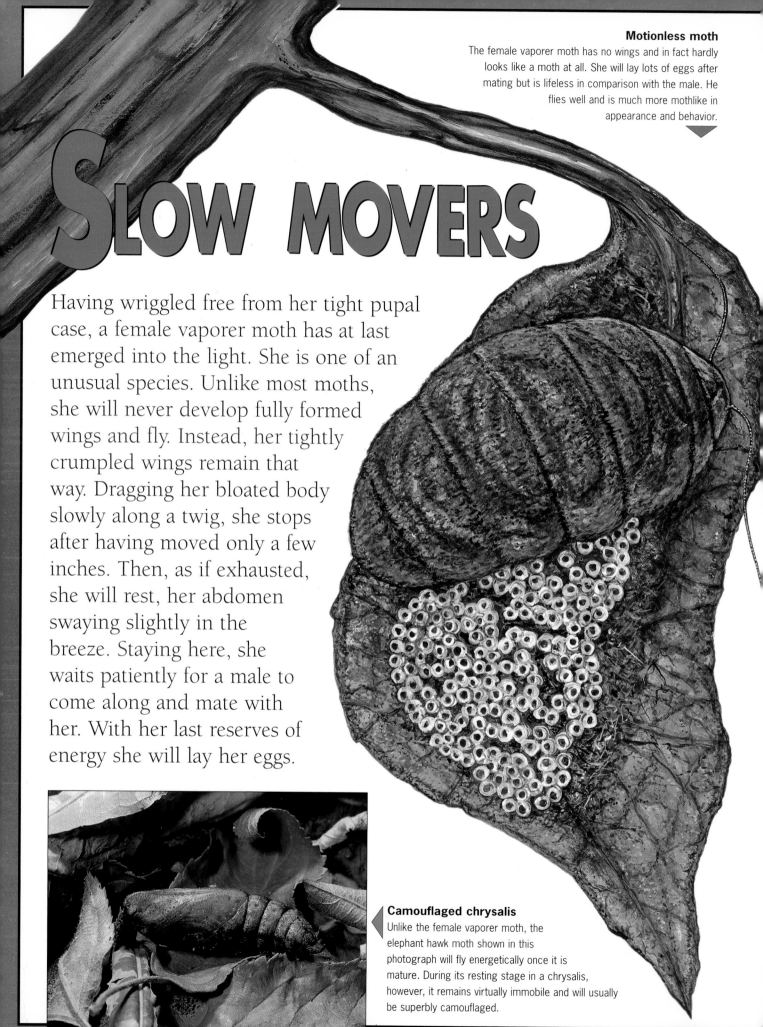

SLOW MOVERS

Having wriggled free from her tight pupal case, a female vaporer moth has at last emerged into the light. She is one of an unusual species. Unlike most moths, she will never develop fully formed wings and fly. Instead, her tightly crumpled wings remain that way. Dragging her bloated body slowly along a twig, she stops after having moved only a few inches. Then, as if exhausted, she will rest, her abdomen swaying slightly in the breeze. Staying here, she waits patiently for a male to come along and mate with her. With her last reserves of energy she will lay her eggs.

Camouflaged chrysalis
Unlike the female vaporer moth, the elephant hawk moth shown in this photograph will fly energetically once it is mature. During its resting stage in a chrysalis, however, it remains virtually immobile and will usually be superbly camouflaged.

At home in a dead holly stump, this stag beetle larva has
no real legs as yet and so can only wriggle along very
slowly, feeding on the wood as it tunnels its way through.

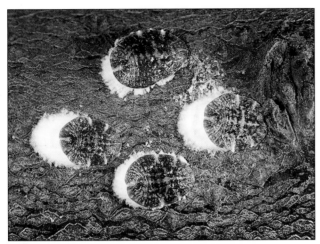

▲ **Just like fixtures**

Photographed on a bay tree, female
scale insects hardly move at all and
remain attached to their host plant. The males, however,
which are not often seen, are a little more active.

Some insects hardly seem to move at all.
Stick insects, for example, will usually
remain immobile by day, restricting
any movement to after dark, when
they are less likely to be spotted and
so can feed without risk of attack. Even if they
are accidentally knocked off a branch, by the wind perhaps, they simply
fall to the ground and lie still, refusing to draw attention to themselves.

CRAWLING ALONG

The larvae of some beetles are also slow movers. They have no legs at all and
so can only wriggle along as they chew tunnels through the wood in which
they live. Fly maggots have no legs either. Like wood beetles, they have no
need to move quickly. The eggs will normally have been laid on a food supply
such as rotting meat or dung, so that they do not have to hunt for a source of
nourishment. Such lack of movement at this early stage in their lives makes it
all the more surprising that they will eventually become speedy fliers.

Caterpillars, too, can be slow movers, working their way along by releasing
one pair of legs at a time and then pushing themselves forward with a
wavelike movement. The chrysalises that they become before the adult moth
or butterfly stage, however, are generally completely immobile. Some
chrysalises, however, move if a predator threatens them.

Slow-moving insects will often have difficulty in escaping from
predators. Some manage to find a way around this. Scale insects, for
instance, will secrete a waxy substance. This coats their backs and makes
them look very unappetizing.

Still as a stick ▶

Native to the island of Madagascar, this giant stick insect remains absolutely
stationary by day as it imitates the plants around it. If disturbed, however, it will
suddenly open its wings with a noise that sounds like paper being crumpled.

HABITATS

You will find them in the sun-baked sands of a desert, as well as in tropical jungles. They abound in open grasslands and populate the banks of ponds and streams. Others, meanwhile, prefer the cool, dark atmosphere of caves or can be classified as swamp-lovers. Because of their small size and adaptability, insects have spread all across our planet with only the deepest oceans and polar regions almost free of them. A number are even city-dwellers, invading our homes at times or using the human body as a habitat. Some would go so far as to lay their tiny eggs in an open wound, if given half a chance, or might opt to set up home in our hair!

Throughout the pages that follow we take you on a guided world tour of all the places where insects are likely to thrive and examine how, in the first place, they came to colonize particular environments. It is an exciting journey, and one that is also full of surprises.

Underground life

Maggots thrive on garden refuse during this important growing stage. But there are likely to be lots of other insects, too, hidden away in a compost heap or burrows. We go digging for them on pages 102-103. There are even some that will tunnel furiously to find a home.

In the kitchen

If you leave food uncovered or floors unswept, insects such as cockroaches may soon infest your home, and come to regard it as their habitat. Some of these tiny creatures can spread terrible diseases and are very unwelcome lodgers.

Underwater

Some insects, as described on pages 110-111, spend their entire larval and pupal stages underwater, only emerging as adults to live in the air or on the ground.

In the jungle

What sort of insects live in a jungle environment? Are they easy to find? And why might many of them be in danger of becoming extinct? Find out on pages 106-107.

Nit picking

The head louse egg, or nit, left, is cemented onto a human hair. Adult human head lice lay as many as 80-100 eggs in their lifetime.

On your body

Jane was trying to concentrate on what her teacher was saying; but every now and then she became distracted by an intense irritation on her scalp. The more she scratched, the worse it got. Little did she know that her head had become home to a family of blood-sucking lice. Last week she had borrowed Emily's comb. Maybe that had something to do with it.

Get out of my hair!

If your scalp starts to itch, get someone to take a careful look. Nits are sometimes visible as tiny yellow lumps along the hairline behind the ears. They hatch so quickly that two weeks later, they will produce a new generation. Special shampoos will help get rid of them.

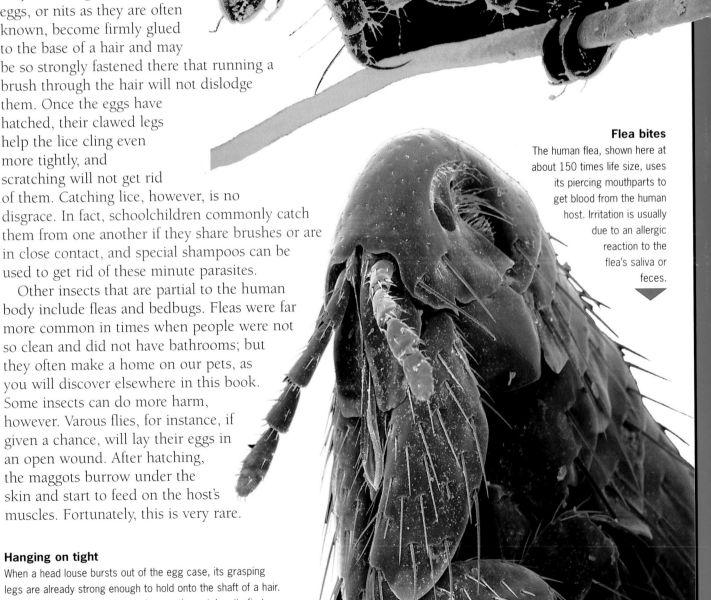

Frantic feeders

Parasitic bedbugs like those shown here need a regular diet of blood and feed on the human body at night if they get into an unclean bed. The bites produce swellings of the skin and can be painful. During the day they lurk in mattresses, on the floor, or inside upholstered furniture.

Minimonsters

The habitat of this louse is again a hairy one, but it is adult pubic regions that it likes best. It feeds on blood fives times every day and is spread by sexual contact if hygiene is poor or by dirty clothing or bedding. It climbs and swings through hairs and locks into position if disturbed by scratching. In this false-color scanning electron micrograph it has been enlarged 20 times.

Lice like to live on our heads, finding it warm and cozy in among our hair. Their eggs, or nits as they are often known, become firmly glued to the base of a hair and may be so strongly fastened there that running a brush through the hair will not dislodge them. Once the eggs have hatched, their clawed legs help the lice cling even more tightly, and scratching will not get rid of them. Catching lice, however, is no disgrace. In fact, schoolchildren commonly catch them from one another if they share brushes or are in close contact, and special shampoos can be used to get rid of these minute parasites.

Other insects that are partial to the human body include fleas and bedbugs. Fleas were far more common in times when people were not so clean and did not have bathrooms; but they often make a home on our pets, as you will discover elsewhere in this book. Some insects can do more harm, however. Varous flies, for instance, if given a chance, will lay their eggs in an open wound. After hatching, the maggots burrow under the skin and start to feed on the host's muscles. Fortunately, this is very rare.

Flea bites

The human flea, shown here at about 150 times life size, uses its piercing mouthparts to get blood from the human host. Irritation is usually due to an allergic reaction to the flea's saliva or feces.

Hanging on tight

When a head louse bursts out of the egg case, its grasping legs are already strong enough to hold onto the shaft of a hair. It will crawl toward the scalp and, once there, takes its first meal of fresh blood. Large numbers, however, only build up in unsanitary conditions. Head lice can cause a lot of discomfort and may also be carriers of the disease typhus.

Meals of blood
A cat flea's stylet pierces the skin, left, and draws up blood. It will frequently feed so greedily that it can go for up to six months between meals.

From host to host
Fleas are fond of leaping around and will jump onto other cats, dogs, or birds if there is close contact. Pet owners need to ensure that baskets or other types of bedding are kept clean and free from these irritating little insects.

ON YOUR PETS

Two small kittens crawl sleepily into their basket. As they do so, tiny insects start to stir. Their sensitive antennae have picked up the warmth of the kittens' bodies and also the gas in their breath. Suddenly, one by one, a dozen fleas leap into the air before tumbling down onto one of the kittens. Soon they will jump from there onto its companion.

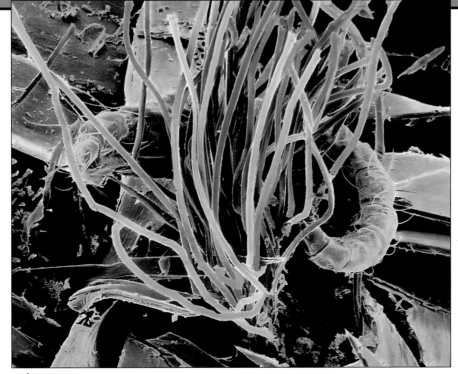

Bird-biters
Birds provide an attractive habitat for some fleas. In this photograph, one is clinging to a feather. Lice, too, sometimes settle in among plumage and cause intense discomfort.

A carpetful of cat fleas
Colored yellow in this photomicrograph, a cat flea larva has coiled itself around the fibers of a carpet. It feeds on waste matter, especially the feces of adult fleas, which are rich in undigested blood. Most of a cat flea's life is spent off the host; but once on a victim, it will suck relentlessly.

There are very few animals that are not annoyed by parasitic insects at some time. So it is no wonder that by bringing pets indoors, we also bring unwanted visitors into the home. Fleas are the most common parasite. They will lay their eggs in places where a pet spends most of its time, cat and dog baskets being favorite spots. The eggs are very tough and may remain unhatched for six months or more. The larvae of fleas are good survivors, too, and will feed on a wide range of foods, including flakes of pets' skin and the droppings of adult fleas.

Vets are able to recommend suitable treatment for pets with fleas. But it is as well to remember that larvae can wander some distance from a pet's usual resting place and may often be found at the edges of a carpet. Eggs may have been laid here, since it is often darker, damper, and less clean than other areas.

Puppy love
Not only do dog fleas bite their hosts and suck up blood, they can also act as a host for tapeworms. Dog fleas have no real eyes. Instead, they have photosensitive spots on the surface of their heads.

Collaring fleas
If you have a dog and notice that it is scratching a lot or see red patches or lumps on its skin, be sure to see the vet. Wearing a flea collar can sometimes keep these parasites at bay.

UNDERGROUND

In the heart of an ant colony strange creatures are hanging from the roof of a chamber. Their bodies have become huge and bloated to such an extent that they look too gross to budge and are in fact entirely immobile. When a few small ants emerge into this chamber, they begin to tap delicately at some of these forms – an action that produces, in just a few seconds, a bright amber drop of liquid from the tip of each swollen abdomen. Greedily, the ants suck up this golden nectar and then rush off, leaving the "living larders" hanging motionless in this miniature subterranean city.

Secret hideaway
Field crickets, like the one below, live in the undergrowth and burrow into holes. Here they are protected from excessive humidity, the chilly air when night falls, and predators. The females will lay their eggs in the soil, too.

Life in a burrow

Some cockroaches do not live in our homes, in warehouses, or in other buildings but prefer the outdoor life. Giant burrowing cockroach females, for instance, are very good mothers and stay underground with their young for as long as nine months, until they can fend for themselves.

Tunneling tiger

Somewhere in West Africa, the tiger beetle larva, right, is tunneling its way through an underground vertical burrow. The egg from which it recently hatched had been laid in the shade of a plant. It will pupate underground, too, and only emerge as an adult.

Stand in any garden or any field, and chances are that right underneath where you are standing there is a great deal of activity going on, even though on the surface it may seem peaceful enough. Below ground, whole communities of insects, each adapted to life in the soil, are going about their daily lives. Here, they feel safely hidden away from predators; and the temperature and humidity remain fairly constant so that there is little danger of freezing or drying out. Even some insects that live as adults above ground were below the ground until maturity. In fact, there are some species that will lay into a hole and then cover their eggs with a plug of soil or froth that they make. Later, when the eggs have hatched, their larvae will need to work their way upward to force an exit to the outside world.

Digging for a home

A thread-waisted wasp from Spain digs a burrow in the sand and will later bring several insects that she has stung so that they become immobile. When her offspring hatch, they can feed on them.

Meet the repletes

In some underground ant colonies – those of the honeypot ants, for example – there are ants that never crawl but simply hang from the roof. All they ever do is act as storehouses for food. Known as repletes (meaning "the full ones"), they have huge bodies that are swollen with sugary liquid. It is excreted so that the other ants can suck it up.

IN GRASSLANDS

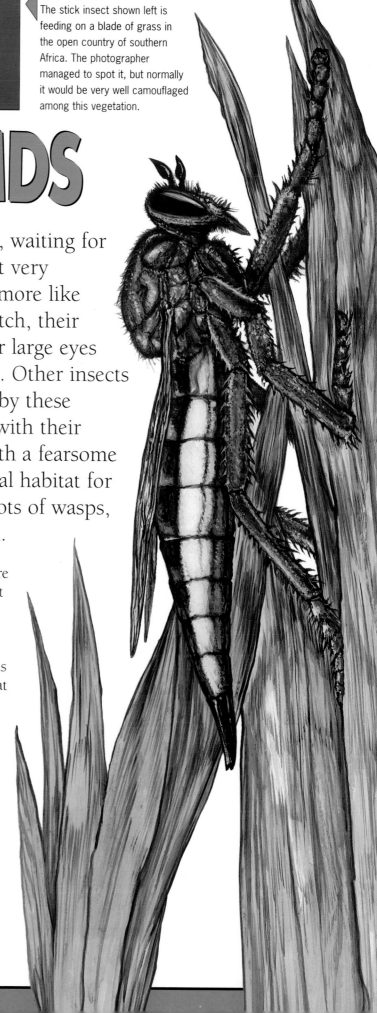

Two robberflies are lurking on stems, waiting for likely prey to pass. Their name is not very accurate, however, because they are more like killers than thieves. As they keep watch, their heads turn every now and then, their large eyes providing them with excellent vision. Other insects stand little chance when confronted by these terrors. They will grab their victims with their powerful legs and then stab them with a fearsome proboscis. Grasslands provide an ideal habitat for these hairy flies, since there will be lots of wasps, bees, beetles, and dragonflies around.

We often hear that insects from a jungle habitat are fast decreasing in numbers or even becoming extinct because of the clearing of rainforests for timber and settlements. But much of the world's grassland is disappearing, too, as more and more highways and railways are built. It would be catastrophic to lose, as a result of this, such creatures as the field cricket that often sings so beautifully all night in summer in his quest for a female.

There is considerable activity at grass-roots level, too. Tiger beetle larvae, for instance, will sit at the entrance to their tunnels, awaiting a victim, such as a meadow ant, on which to pounce. Their prey will then be dragged into the holes. The adults can fly and may be seen in meadows during the summer, attacking beetles, ants, or caterpillars.

Butterflies also abound in grasslands, as do many insects that would gladly make a meal of them – the strangely named wart-biter cricket, for example, that feeds on live prey as well as vegetation and seeds. You can recognize a wart-biter cricket by its distinctive sound – a series of clicks.

Ladybug pupae
Two pupae rest on blades of grass and will soon become more recognizable as ladybugs. Wherever there are meadows or grassland, these members of the beetle family thrive, feeding on small, soft insects.

Ruthless robbers
Fast-moving predators, robberflies will hide in the grass and then pounce on their victims. Some species are even as successful hunters as the dragonflies.

Grassland omnivore
The giant weta from New Zealand feeds on plants and fungi but will also eat flies and even any rat feces that it finds among the brush.

Meadow music
Meadow grasshoppers, like the one below, are usually well hidden, so that the only way you would know they are there is if you heard them making their characteristic sounds, or if you caught sight of one while it was jumping.

IN THE JUNGLE

A sudden movement catches the eye of a passing moon rat. It has spotted a jungle nymph that immediately rubs its wings together, curls its abdomen into a defensive display, and then stabs its sharp spines into the predator's nose. With a shriek the rat rushes off to find a less troublesome meal.

It has been estimated that there are probably millions of different species of insects living in the tropical rainforests of our planet. However, if you were to look around such jungles, you would be lucky to spot a single one at first. Many are extremely well camouflaged and others may be high up in the canopy. Insects of the jungle vary in size from wasps smaller than the period at the end of this sentence to butterflies with wingspans almost as wide as this book. Sadly, though, many of these insects, and possibly some never discovered, are being wiped out as more and more tropical forest is cut down for timber or for conversion to farmland.

Winged beauty
A birdwing butterfly in the photograph above is emerging from its magnificent gold-colored chrysalis in the heart of the Indonesian jungle.

Live thorns
Disguised as part of the vegetation of a South American rainforest area, these thorn bugs hardly look like a life form at all.

A forest fungus beetle
This so-called pleasing fungus beetle is from the Amazon rainforest in Ecuador.

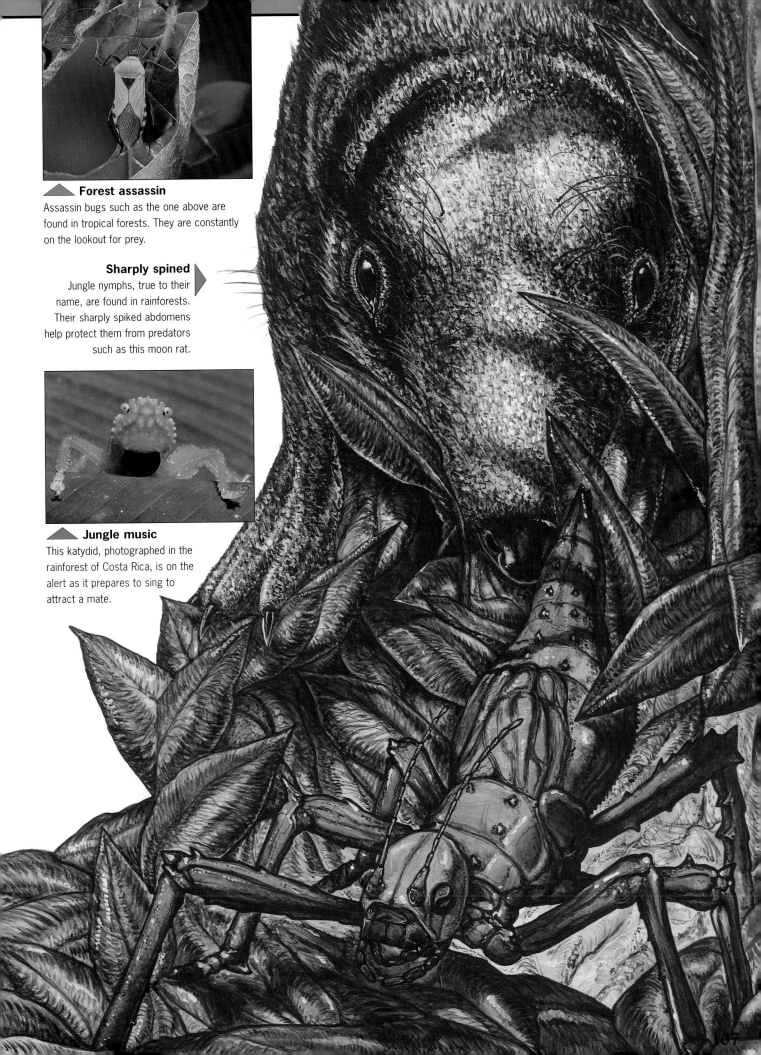

Forest assassin

Assassin bugs such as the one above are found in tropical forests. They are constantly on the lookout for prey.

Sharply spined

Jungle nymphs, true to their name, are found in rainforests. Their sharply spiked abdomens help protect them from predators such as this moon rat.

Jungle music

This katydid, photographed in the rainforest of Costa Rica, is on the alert as it prepares to sing to attract a mate.

IN THE DESERT

A large female tarantula, deep in her desert burrow, has picked up the delicate vibrations of a calling male. However, on reaching the entrance, there is no sign of him. Instead, a huge, black shiny wasp suddenly leaps on top of her. The tarantula shows her fangs, but the wasp is too quick and stings her. The venom will now spread rapidly through the tarantula's nervous system, and the wasp will be able to drag her back to its burrow to lay a single egg on her flesh. When the larva hatches, it will slowly eat the tarantula alive.

During the day deserts look lifeless, since few forms of life venture out in the relentless sun. But, as night draws on, a surprising number of insects suddenly appear. Many of them hide away at the hottest times because they are small and tend to dry out very quickly if exposed to extremely high temperatures. However, a few tough species do come out by day – among them the desert ants. They choose to be active at a time when there are fewer predators around and when there is therefore less competition for food. Rain may come to certain deserts only once every few years. Sea fog blown inland, however, can sometimes provide moisture.

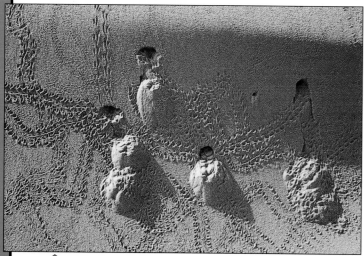

Beetle burrows

In the photograph above, taken in the Mohave Desert of Arizona, beetle burrows are clearly visible in the sand. You can also see the insect tracks that lead to and from them.

Scarabs in the sand

Scarab beetles, like the one shown right, were thought to be gods by the ancient Egyptians. It was even believed that they rolled the sun around the sky.

Cooling down

In an attempt to keep cool, darkling beetles, such as the one in the illustration below, raise themselves off the sandy ground.

Taken by surprise
The tarantula hawk wasp, below, frequents the arid regions of Mexico and likes to feed on any nectar it can find among the desert plants. The females will sting tarantulas and paralyze them so that their larvae can feed on these spiders. Trapdoor spiders often fall victim to these wasps, too, and tend to be stung between their legs.

Catching prey
Carnivorous water crickets are commonly found by ponds and streams where they lurk in the hope of catching small insects that fall into the water.

Strong swimmer
Waterboatmen come regularly to the surface to replenish their supply of air. Many types of waterplants and algae form the major part of their diet.

BY PONDS AND

On a sunny day by the side of a large stream of cool water, dragonflies are skimming over the surface through the reeds. Among them are species – known collectively as hawkers – that patrol backward and forward. These exquisitely beautiful creatures are water-lovers and among the swiftest of all the insects. As they hover, dive, or swerve, they beat their wings at up to 30 times per second. Delicate damselflies also populate the waterside; and on the surface, there may be pond-skaters, waterstriders, and whirligig beetles, all providing a fascinating aquatic display.

STREAMS

Water is usually a very stable habitat and will attract many species of insects, even if some only come to drink. A number spend their entire lives in the water, but others are only underwater as larvae before graduating to the ground or the air when fully mature. Mayflies, for instance, may live up to four years underwater, where they swim by wriggling their abdomens up and down, but each spring some emerge in large numbers from lakes, ponds, and streams, usually to die within the day.

Dragonflies will lay their eggs on water weeds by the edge of a stream in mud or actually in the water. When their larvae hatch, they remain underwater for about two years, breathing through their gills, shedding their skin up to 15 times, and hunting by stealth for other kinds of insects and even small fish. Once fully mature and out of the water, they also have short lives and lend color to the water's edge for only around six weeks. They are ferocious predators, in spite of their obvious grace, and hunt on the wing.

Dragonfly territory
The early part of a dragonfly's life is spent underwater, and they stay nearby even when they are flying as adults.

IN COLD CLIMATES

In Northern Canada the temperature will still be low even when winter is nearly over, and tiny insects will scuttle over the ice. When snow scorpionflies wake from their hibernation, they creep along on the lookout for food. At this time of the year there is little around, however.

▲ **Scratching away**

Polar bears will start to scratch if a parasite succeeds in infesting their fur. It is unlikely to be snow fleas that annoy them, however, since they do not feed on blood.

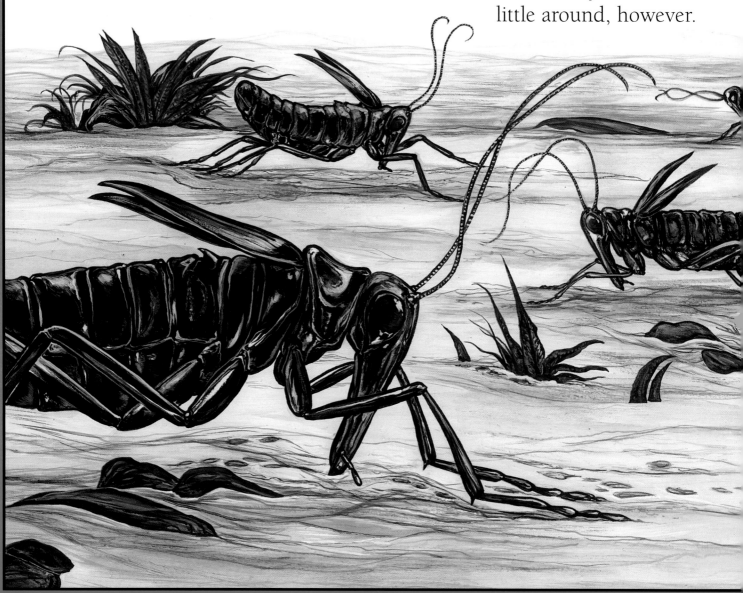

Rare specimen

This snowfield or ice insect is rarely seen and survives on dead aerial plankton and other tiny insects found under stones in the ice.

Insects are cold-blooded creatures. In spite of that, a number are able to live in sub-zero temperatures, frequently with the cooperation of other forms of life. Lice that infest seals, for instance, remain dormant while the mammal is swimming in very cold sea water. Only when the seal comes ashore and radiates body heat will the louse become active and feed.

Other insects rely on each other to get through the worst of bad weather. By gathering in large clusters, many can survive, even if those on the outside perish. But a few remain active without assistance. All they need is a little sunshine, and their dark bodies can absorb enough heat to allow them to hunt, feed, and mate. There are even insects with a form of antifreeze in their blood that prevents it from turning to ice.

Cold-lovers

To pick up an insect known as a rock-crawler would be exceedingly cruel even if you held it gently. They hate the heat, and exposure to the temperature of your hand could kill them.

In the deep freeze

Snow scorpionflies live in the colder parts of North America, and their larvae usually emerge before the winter freeze sets in. They can sometimes be seen hopping across the snow, looking for other insects on which they will feed.

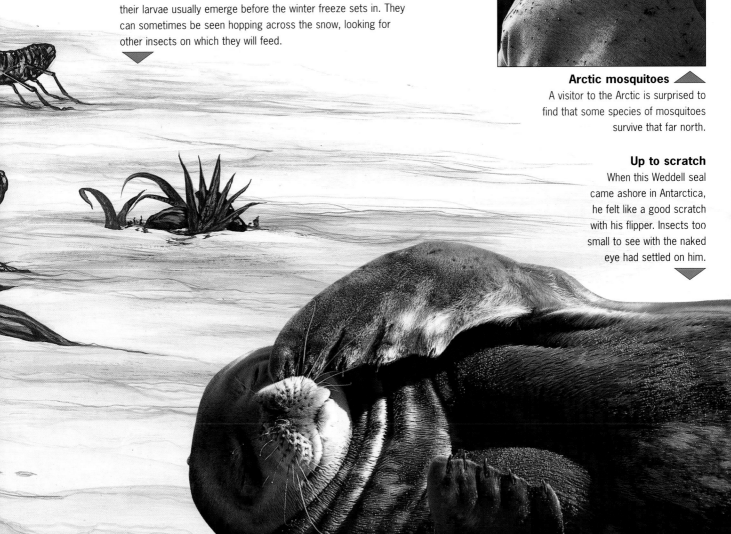

Arctic mosquitoes

A visitor to the Arctic is surprised to find that some species of mosquitoes survive that far north.

Up to scratch

When this Weddell seal came ashore in Antarctica, he felt like a good scratch with his flipper. Insects too small to see with the naked eye had settled on him.

LIFECYCLES

We are born, we grow up, and then many of us go on to have children of our own. For any group of animals to survive, it needs to produce a new generation in this way, and insects are no exception. However, because they are so diverse, their lifecycles can vary considerably.

Insects that need to mate in order to reproduce, for instance, have developed a bewildering range of courtship strategies. A number will sing "love songs," and others will release special perfumes to attract a mate. In a few species, meanwhile, the females can reproduce on their own, without the need for a mate. In several instances, too, young insects go through very distinct stages before they eventually take on their adult form. Some insects care for their young and will defend them with their lives. But not all make good parents. The story of how insects reproduce and the young grow to maturity is one of the most enthralling aspects of natural history.

Young parasites
Some insects lay their eggs either inside or on the larvae of other insects. When the young hatch, they will have a ready food supply and feed like parasites.

The royal egg-layers
Meet the termite queen, together with other insect queens, and discover on pages 128-129 how they live and why they are often so much bigger than the rest of the colony.

Intimate moments
Insects have evolved many different types of courtship rituals to ensure that the sexes get together and produce the next generation, as explained on pages 122-123.

Time to hatch
How does the wasp, right, hatch from its egg? Is it true that some insects take months or even years to hatch? And what are the larvae like that emerge? Turn to pages 130-131 to find out.

LOVE SONGS

A male katydid is trying to attract the attention of a female. Resting on a leaf, he is about to rub his forewings together and will start to make music. Not far away, meanwhile, there is a female who is waiting expectantly. Her hearing organs are hidden away in tiny slits on her limbs, and she is listening for the call of a potential mate. His love song is loud and clear.

Making music
Some katydids make a clicking sound, but others make more of a trill. A few even alternate clicks and trills as they sing. One species actually seems to say the word "katy-did."

A rasping call
Caught on film as he held his wings at an angle to his body to produce his characteristic rasping call, this male cricket will no doubt finally succeed in attracting a female who will give in to his vocal charms.

Seductive tones

The male's calling brought together these two short-horned grasshoppers, photographed in Indonesia, and they promptly mated, as above. The male is the smaller of the two.

There are numbers of insects that chirp, hiss, or sing to attract a partner, and usually it is the males of the species who are the vocalists. But the noise does not always come from their mouths. Instead, other body parts may be used. Most male grasshoppers, for instance, will rub part of their legs against the thickest veins on their outer wings in a process known as *stridulation*.

Each type of grasshopper sings a distinct type of love song, and experts are able to identify different species from their serenades. The faster the stridulation, the higher the sound that is produced. The females of one type of grasshopper do sing – not, however, to attract a mate but to frighten enemies away!

Adult male cicadas are perhaps the keenest singers of all and produce their songs from two organs on either side of the abdomen. Their monotonous callings can sometimes reach a level of decibels that is louder than that produced by a pneumatic drill at full blast.

Hitting a low note
This southern lubber grasshopper from Arizona does not rub its wings together as quickly as some and so hits a lower note.

Turn it down!
Cicadas are undoubtedly among the noisiest members of the insect kingdom and are well known for their loud and rhythmic mating calls.

FIGHTING

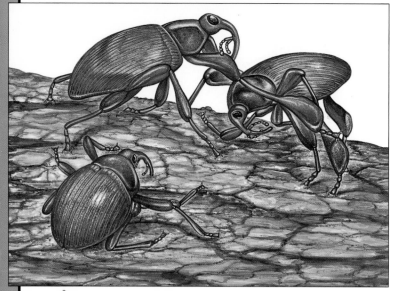

Let battle begin!
Some male weevils from Central America have spectacular forelegs with clubbed ends. They are used in battles against rivals who dare to approach a male's partner as she is about to lay her eggs. It is usually the larger male who wins, but death rarely results.

Their long appendages are locked together as two Australian gladiator flies behave just like stags in the rutting season. One starts to kick the other in the head; and before the dazed insect can react, another violent blow knocks him backward as the two battle over mating with a female.

Soon the weaker fly starts to back away as blow after blow rains down on him. The more powerful fly will now be able to claim rights to the female, who is sitting quietly nearby, and the unfortunate loser will have to take his chances elsewhere. Perhaps he will win another bout.

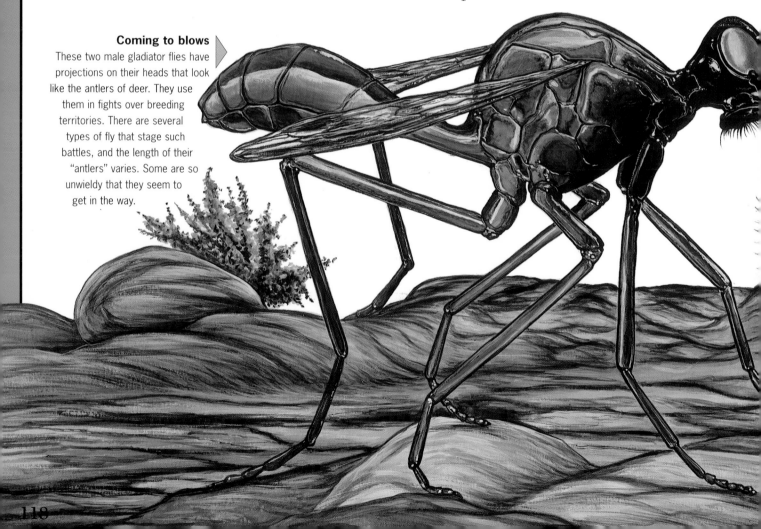

Coming to blows
These two male gladiator flies have projections on their heads that look like the antlers of deer. They use them in fights over breeding territories. There are several types of fly that stage such battles, and the length of their "antlers" varies. Some are so unwieldy that they seem to get in the way.

TO WIN A FEMALE

In the world of insects a male's attempts to reproduce are not over even once he has found a female. Competition between rivals can be very intense, the males of some species performing ritualistic battles. Gladiator flies also fight over territory, using their antlerlike appendages in head-to-heads. An area with lots of crevices where females will be able to lay their eggs is worth fighting for. But such contests usually only last a few seconds because one will be knocked over by the force of his opponent's shoving. Their long, slim, stiltlike legs are not very stable.

However, there is some fairness to such competitions. Gladiator flies first consider the size and strength of an opponent by means of a simple bout of pushing. If one of the flies is much weaker than the other, it will withdraw at this stage and so no battle will take place. If they are more evenly matched, the contest will begin.

MATING FLIGHTS

Levels of activity are high in the nest, and there seems to be chaos as thousands of workers cut exits for their winged brothers and sisters by attacking the walls for all they are worth. Previously, special raised areas had been constructed outside the termite mound for use as launch pads. When the swarm is ready to leave, it will come through the openings in countless numbers. Their flight will be hesitant, however, and they will not go far. Roughly equal numbers of males and females will leave together on such nuptial flights, which last for only up to two hours, and which take place with the start of a rainy period.

There are several types of insect that swarm. Such mating flights usually occur at specific times of the year when conditions are right for egg-laying or nest-building. Swarming greatly increases the chances of finding a mate. However, there is a down side to this. Other animals, especially birds and bats, tend to home in on swarms and will feast on some of its members.

In a mosquito swarm there will be lots of males and fewer females, and so a lot of competition arises, since a female mosquito usually only likes to mate once, and even then will not always be willing. Mayflies also swarm before mating. The males soar to a high level and then descend, looking upward for a suitable female. The females fly into the swarm and are grabbed by the males from below. Mating occurs in flight and is over very quickly.

After the summer rains
In South Africa, after the summer rains have slowed, winged termites – surrounded by far smaller workers – start to emerge. Their nuptial flight is about to begin; but before founding new colonies, or when they reenter an existing one, they will bite off their own wings.

Countless flies
Hundreds of tiny bristly dance flies can be seen here as they mate on the wing. The males all gathered and then waited for the females to fly into their swarm. Some species bring the females nuptial gifts of prey and even wrap them up in frothy secretions.

Bee swarms
Giant honeybees like these from southern India gather in vast numbers when they swarm. It is dazzling to watch them move in a buzzing mass and then fly to a tree to rest. Always stay out of the way of such a swarm for fear of being stung.

Out of the tower
Winged termites from various mounds that are near each other join in one huge, synchronized swarm. It ensures interbreeding between different colonies. Workers make holes in the mounds through which the alates, or winged termites, can fly free.

Surfacing
At a precise season some termite nymphs become winged. Gradually, as this photograph shows, they start to mill around before leaving their underground residence in a great swarm for the mating flight.

121

GETTING TOGETHER

The mating wheel
Male and female damselflies contort their bodies when mating, as in this illustration. It even looks as if they are somehow harnessed together. They stay like this for a while and sometimes fly around in tandem. The female then lays her fertilized eggs in water, and the male is so chivalrous that he helps his mate onto dry land again by hauling her up.

Resting on a twig, a male and female damselfly are in the process of mating. This male is lucky. He might not have found a partner. There are always many more male damselflies, so that only about fifty percent of males ever succeed in mating. Female damselflies, however, may mate several times during their lives.

Take your partner
Two stag beetles have been caught on camera as the male mounts the female and they start to mate. These beetles get their name from the large antennaelike mandibles of the males.

Pairing off
Even insects with a name like stink locusts, given to them because of the foul-smelling liquid they can secrete to deter predators, get together to mate. As you can see in this photograph, the male is a lot smaller than the female and sits astride her. She will soon lay her fertilized eggs.

End to end ▲
Also known as mayflies, this species of cockchafer beetle mates with the tips of their abdomens touching, end to end, as in the picture above. They do considerable damage to trees and crops, as do their larvae.

Insects have developed many different ways of making sure that the two sexes meet. Some, such as silk moths, use scents, known as *pheromones*, to attract a mate. Others sing to each other to attract attention, form huge swarms, or use a local source of food, such as a cow pat, as a rendezvous. A few will bring each other nuptial gifts. Male dance flies, for example, will offer the females their prey, and this gift is sometimes a rival male. But the females are often fussy; and if the quality of a gift is not adequate, they may reject a male's advances. Some entomologists have also suggested that a few male dance flies deceive in the process of courtship by trying to fob off their partners with a substitute gift of seeds instead of a meal that is sufficient to satisfy a carnivorous appetite. Sometimes, though, it is visual signals that are important. Wing displays may act as sexual advertisements in some grasshoppers, for instance, while others seem to recognize each other by their color and patterning. For insects that are out and about when it is light, this form of courtship is highly effective.

Intimate moments ▷
This pair of seven-spot ladybugs is in the process of mating. The male and female are both good runners and voracious aphid-hunters, and can squirt nasty fluids at enemies.

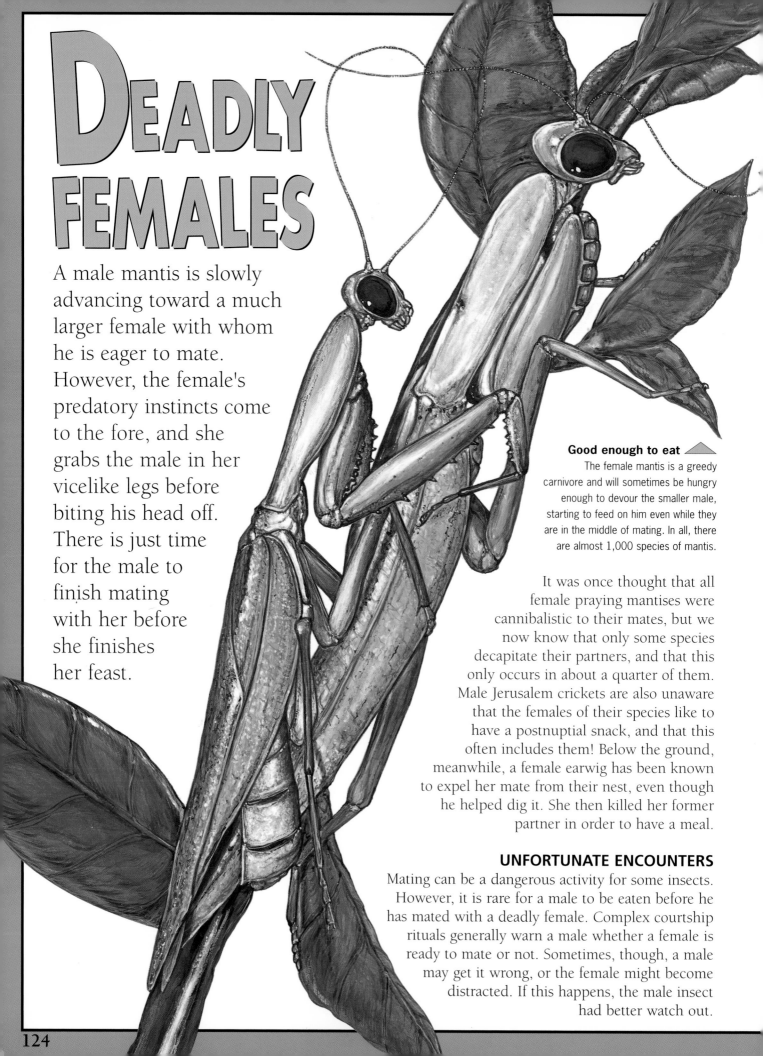

DEADLY FEMALES

A male mantis is slowly advancing toward a much larger female with whom he is eager to mate. However, the female's predatory instincts come to the fore, and she grabs the male in her vicelike legs before biting his head off. There is just time for the male to finish mating with her before she finishes her feast.

Good enough to eat
The female mantis is a greedy carnivore and will sometimes be hungry enough to devour the smaller male, starting to feed on him even while they are in the middle of mating. In all, there are almost 1,000 species of mantis.

It was once thought that all female praying mantises were cannibalistic to their mates, but we now know that only some species decapitate their partners, and that this only occurs in about a quarter of them. Male Jerusalem crickets are also unaware that the females of their species like to have a postnuptial snack, and that this often includes them! Below the ground, meanwhile, a female earwig has been known to expel her mate from their nest, even though he helped dig it. She then killed her former partner in order to have a meal.

UNFORTUNATE ENCOUNTERS
Mating can be a dangerous activity for some insects. However, it is rare for a male to be eaten before he has mated with a deadly female. Complex courtship rituals generally warn a male whether a female is ready to mate or not. Sometimes, though, a male may get it wrong, or the female might become distracted. If this happens, the male insect had better watch out.

Making a meal of him
A male and female praying mantis have mated one morning in the jungle of Southeast Asia, and as you can see, the female is now eating her mate for breakfast. She is larger than her mate, and so the unfortunate male does not stand a chance. He is speedily devoured.

Too hungry to stop
The female praying mantis is such a skillful hunter and so hungry most of the time that she will continue to catch prey, such as a cicada, even when mating, as you can see in this photograph. If she had not caught this cicada, she might have eaten her mate, as in the remarkable picture shown top right.

THE NEXT GENERATION

Entomologists have suggested that when a female mantis kills and eats her mate, it is a way of ensuring that she is sufficiently well nourished to produce healthy eggs. She is very skilled at grabbing many sorts of prey – including her partner – with strong legs that are armed with spikes. The female mantis also has a very long reach with these sawlike legs and is more likely to succeed than a male mantis when hunting because she is larger overall.

Some mosquitoes also number among them cannibalistic females that eat their mates. They go for the males' heads and then drain them dry. The only thing these greedy females leave behind is a husk that will break away. The males even seem to make themselves available quite willingly as meals for the females, who may strike at their partners even when they are in the middle of mating.

Queen bees are potential killers, too, and will not hesitate to use their stingers against a rival. There can only be one queen in a colony of bees. They also cause death in another way because, after mating, the drones or males will usually be driven out to starve. In another strange form of behavior female Mormon crickets of western North America actually do battle with each other over the males, but usually it is the males of the animal kingdom that fight with each other over females.

Dinner comes later
Two robberflies are mating here, but will the male survive? Male robberflies have to be careful, since the females often attack if they are approached too quickly for their liking.

EGG-LAYING

Resting now, a female alderfly has just laid her eggs on the underside of a leaf. She is not a true fly in spite of her name but belongs to the same order as snake and lacewing flies. There are well over 200 eggs in this batch. Several females have laid their eggs close together, so that the plant will probably become weighed down by them all. The plant is by the waterside; so when the larvae eventually crawl out, they will be able to feed on aquatic insects. The alderfly larvae's gills will help them breathe underwater while they seek out their prey. They have powerful jaws and can give a victim a nasty bite.

In clumps
The tiny white eggs shown above have been laid in a great mass by a female horsefly. They are neatly stacked and closely packed in tiers on a rush. The eggs are usually to be found near water, which is the habitat of the larvae that hatch from them.

126

Into the water
This golden-colored hawker dragonfly was photographed in central England and is busy ovipositing, or egg-laying, directly into the water where its larvae will hatch.

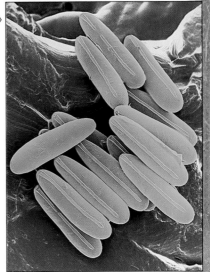

Most insects are *oviparous*, which means that they lay eggs from which young will hatch. The shape and size of these eggs can vary greatly from one group of insects to another. Many produce large numbers of eggs, laying them near a source of food and then leaving them to hatch by themselves. Occasionally, the adult female builds a form of cocoon, or *ootheca*, for them. In other instances the eggs are simply scattered with a careless flick of the abdomen.

Other insects lay fewer eggs and take more care where they are laid. The females may stay with the eggs until they hatch and may even continue to guard the larvae for a short time afterward. However, in the case of predatory insects this form of maternal care has definite time limits, and those young that do not disperse speedily enough may possibly end up as their mother's lunch.

Some insects, however, are never parted from their eggs because they are *ovoviviparous* and retain them inside their own bodies until they hatch. The eggs do not gain any nutrition from the mother, but there are other advantages to this form of reproduction. They will be protected from the approach of predators and parasites, as well as from poor weather conditions.

Under a potato plant's leaf
A Colorado beetle has just completed egg-laying on the underside of a potato leaf in the photograph below. Its eggs are orange and slightly elongated in shape. Colorado beetles produce either one or two generations each year.

On a stem
This tawny cockroach from Europe is carrying her egg sac with her as she climbs along a stem. The sac protrudes from her rear, as you can see, and probably contains about 10 eggs. After carrying the sac for a day or so, she will deposit it in a dark spot and then abandon it. Other species of cockroach are more maternal, however, and remain with their young.

Head of the colony

This termite queen is being fed by her many workers. She cannot find food for herself and lives mostly on her workers' saliva, which is rich in proteins.

THE ROLE OF

A queen termite has been trapped inside a cell so small that she cannot even turn around in it and will remain here until she dies. However, she is extremely well fed and cared for.

Big and bloated

A queen termite, as you can see here, is huge in comparison with the workers and soldiers that surround her. She is in fact like an enormous egg-laying machine. Within her royal apartments in the mounds a queen may lay as many as 35,000 eggs in a day and so several million in a year. She is the only insect queen with a king who mates and lives with her.

Social insects, such as termites, bees, wasps, and ants, are among the most important forms of life on earth; and wherever they are found, they play a vital role in our environment, joining together to form what is sometimes called a *superorganism*. It is the presence of a queen that keeps all the individuals within an insect colony working closely together as a unit.

Queens are always female and emerge from fertilized eggs. If a replacement is needed, she will be selected from newly hatched larvae and then fed on a very rich diet. In honeybees it will be a substance known as *royal jelly*. It is high in sugars and growth-promoting chemicals. A queen honey bee is about twice the size of other bees in a hive and may live for four or five years longer than the rest of the colony. She rarely leaves the hive except for mating, when she flies out to attract drones by her scent.

Time to lay

The queen honeybee, seen centrally, is in the middle of egg-laying. She backs into each cell and lays one egg, the size of a pinhead, in each, sticking it in place.

Ladies-in-waiting

The weaver ant queen in this photograph taken in West Africa is entirely surrounded by attentive female workers who look after all the needs of the head of the colony. Her "ladies-in-waiting" see that she is fed and well protected.

THE QUEEN

Her many diligent daughters, the workers, see to her every need. After all, without the queen the colony would slowly fall into decline.

LIFE AT THE TOP

In general, queens do very little work apart from mating and laying eggs, since it is the workers' responsibility to care for the larvae and to collect food. It is a new young queen wasp, however, who is responsible for starting a paper nest from pieces of dry wood. Among certain wasps, if several establish a nest, they will fight until one is shown to be dominant. She becomes the queen and will continue to show who is boss by attacking them at intervals, frequently also eating their eggs in a display of aggression. If she is deposed, she will drop all the way down to the bottom of the hierarchy.

In ant colonies only the males and new, or virgin, queens have wings. But once their mating flights are over, the queens will bite off their wings before starting a new colony. They will not fly again.

Royal body language ▷

This hornet queen has adopted a defensive posture. Normally she will not attack; but if the nest is threatened by intruders, she will pull her weight and defend it aggressively. It is she who begins the building of a nest from pulp. The first generation usually has only female workers. Unfertilized eggs laid in late summer produce males.

TIME TO HATCH

One spring day there is sudden activity on the surface of a leaf as a new generation of ladybugs is about to hatch. Lots of eggs have been laid in batches, and they are so tiny that it is hard to believe they could contain live larvae that have developed inside them over the course of a week. The cap at the top of each egg is now pushed through as the larvae within try to crawl out. They look nothing like mature ladybugs at this stage but are greedy carnivores and will start to feed on aphids, possibly as many as 20 per day each. There are other species of ladybugs, however, that are herbivores and feed on nothing but foliage. The prickly covering of the larvae gives them protection from predators as they eat away at clover and other plants.

◢◣ Wriggling out
These tiny caterpillars of the buff-tip moth are starting to crawl out of their eggs. Some shells are already empty, as you can see.

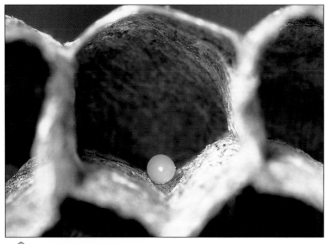

◢◣ Inside a wasp's nest cell
In the first of a series of four photographs, you can see the tiny, round, white egg that has been laid at the base of a hexagonal cell in the nest of a Polistes wasp.

◢◣ Biting through
In the second picture in this sequence, a fully formed adult wasp is biting open the lid of its cell, and one antenna is poking through. It probably requires a lot of effort for the wasp to work its way out.

When it is time to hatch, some insects simply bite their way through a soft membrane. Others, however, have to struggle quite hard to escape from their eggs; while for those that are buried underground, the later journey to the surface may prove a difficult one, especially if the earth has become dry and hard. However, many eggs only hatch when environmental conditions are just right, so lots of potential problems are avoided.

The eggs of stick insects can take months or even years to hatch. However, the young do not have to fight their way out of the eggs as some insects do. When the nymph is ready to face the world, a small trapdoor at one end, known as the *operculum*, pops open, and the stick insect can come out from the confines of the shell.

▲ Opening time

Looking nothing at all like the ladybugs that they will eventually become, these spined larvae that look more like small brushes have just hatched. The eggs were laid on foliage, and the larvae will now feed on aphids before pupating. As adults they will continue to feed greedily on these sap-suckers. No wonder ladybugs and their larvae are said to be a gardener's best friend!

▲ Head first

The third shot in this series shows the yellow-and-black head of this wasp, with its two long antennae, coming out of the opened cell. The top of the cell has been removed by the wasp and looks like a cap.

▲ Final exit

In the fourth and final photograph of this sequence, an infertile female worker wasp is now almost out of her cell and ready to face the world. It has been about five weeks since the egg was laid.

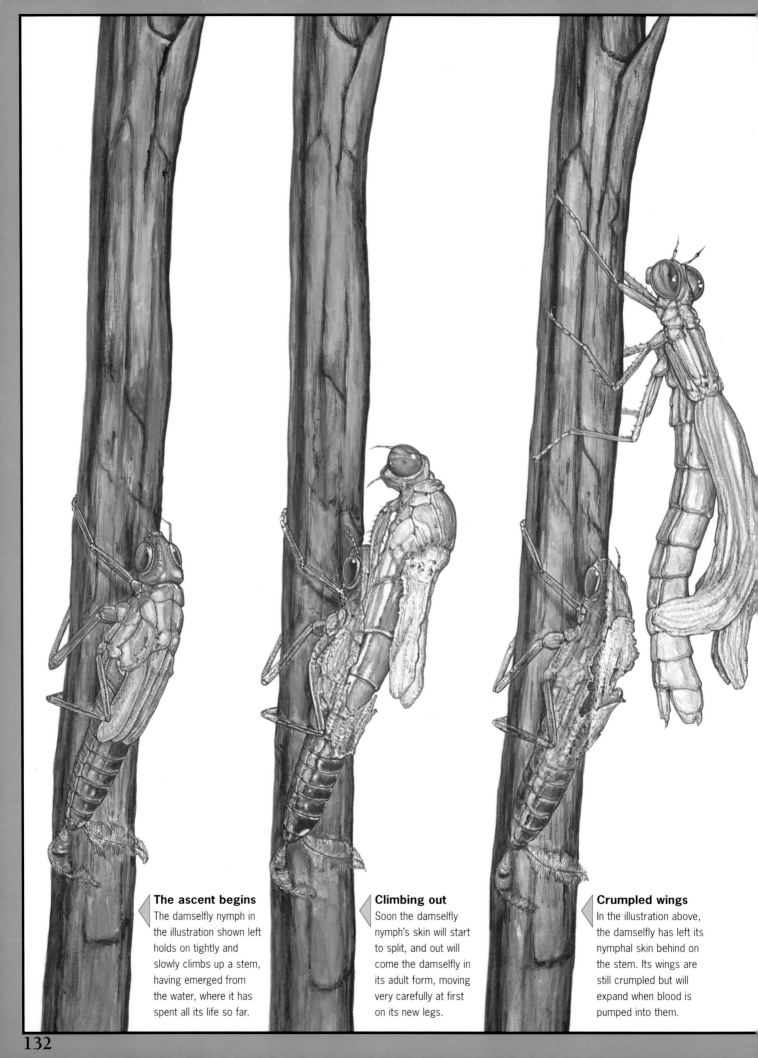

The ascent begins
The damselfly nymph in the illustration shown left holds on tightly and slowly climbs up a stem, having emerged from the water, where it has spent all its life so far.

Climbing out
Soon the damselfly nymph's skin will start to split, and out will come the damselfly in its adult form, moving very carefully at first on its new legs.

Crumpled wings
In the illustration above, the damselfly has left its nymphal skin behind on the stem. Its wings are still crumpled but will expand when blood is pumped into them.

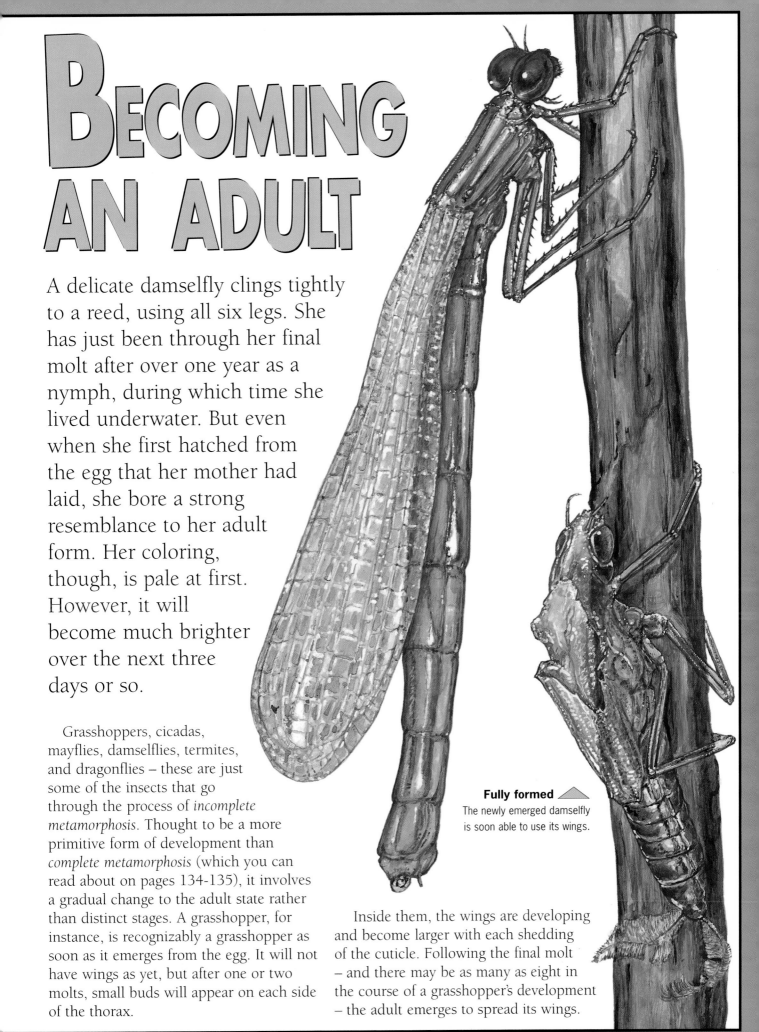

BECOMING AN ADULT

A delicate damselfly clings tightly to a reed, using all six legs. She has just been through her final molt after over one year as a nymph, during which time she lived underwater. But even when she first hatched from the egg that her mother had laid, she bore a strong resemblance to her adult form. Her coloring, though, is pale at first. However, it will become much brighter over the next three days or so.

Grasshoppers, cicadas, mayflies, damselflies, termites, and dragonflies – these are just some of the insects that go through the process of *incomplete metamorphosis*. Thought to be a more primitive form of development than *complete metamorphosis* (which you can read about on pages 134-135), it involves a gradual change to the adult state rather than distinct stages. A grasshopper, for instance, is recognizably a grasshopper as soon as it emerges from the egg. It will not have wings as yet, but after one or two molts, small buds will appear on each side of the thorax.

Fully formed
The newly emerged damselfly is soon able to use its wings.

Inside them, the wings are developing and become larger with each shedding of the cuticle. Following the final molt – and there may be as many as eight in the course of a grasshopper's development – the adult emerges to spread its wings.

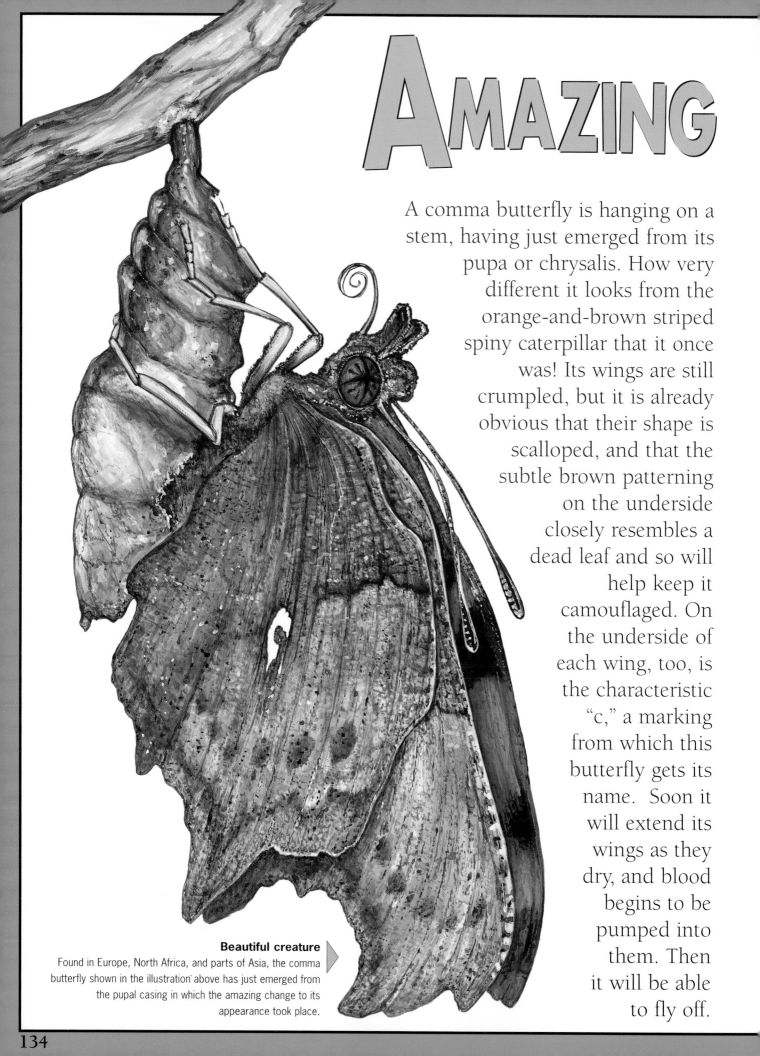

AMAZING

A comma butterfly is hanging on a stem, having just emerged from its pupa or chrysalis. How very different it looks from the orange-and-brown striped spiny caterpillar that it once was! Its wings are still crumpled, but it is already obvious that their shape is scalloped, and that the subtle brown patterning on the underside closely resembles a dead leaf and so will help keep it camouflaged. On the underside of each wing, too, is the characteristic "c," a marking from which this butterfly gets its name. Soon it will extend its wings as they dry, and blood begins to be pumped into them. Then it will be able to fly off.

Beautiful creature
Found in Europe, North Africa, and parts of Asia, the comma butterfly shown in the illustration above has just emerged from the pupal casing in which the amazing change to its appearance took place.

TRANSFORMATIONS

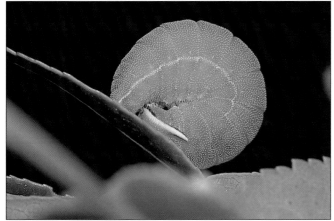

▲ **About to pupate**

In the first of this series of photographs taken over a few days, you can see the larva or caterpillar of a two-tailed pasha butterfly that has been feeding on a strawberry tree. It has now stopped eating and will soon begin to pupate.

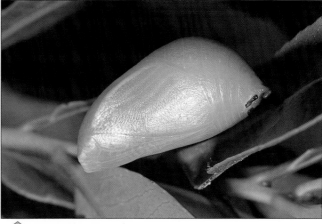

▲ **Resting phase**

In the second picture in this series, having taken on a different form from the caterpillar that it was, the pupa of this two-tailed pasha remains perfectly still until the next stage of its development, as part of the process of complete metamorphosis.

▲ **Coming out of the pupa**

In the third photograph in this series, as you can see, the mature two-tailed pasha is starting to emerge after having metamorphosed to this exquisite new form. Its wings are very crumpled because the butterfly has developed in a very confined space.

▲ **What a difference!**

Shown resting on the pupa from which it has emerged, the two-tailed pasha butterfly from tropical Africa has now stretched its wings and is finally about to fly free. It has completely transformed from the caterpillar that it once was, top left.

A month previously, after eating its own eggshell, which was full of valuable nutrients, a tiny caterpillar started to wriggle along a twig in search of more food. Its appetite was insatiable. It ate and ate, shedding its skin each time it became too big for it. Then, one day, when it could feed no more, the caterpillar began to spin a small patch of silk on the underside of a leaf. Grasping this with its last pair of legs, the caterpillar shed its larval skin for the last time. It now became a pupa, and in a few days the butterfly would emerge.

When you were born, you had some resemblance to an adult. Insects that undergo *complete metamorphosis* start life looking nothing at all like their parents. However many times the larva sheds its skin, it does not become any more like the mature form until a miraculous change takes place inside the pupa. Once it emerges as an adult, it will not grow any more because it can never shed its exoskeleton. Bees, wasps, ants, beetles, butterflies, and moths all undergo complete metamorphosis.

Born free
A tsetse fly female can be seen here as she deposits a larva. Tsetse flies only produce one egg at a time and look after it internally until the larva is ready to emerge from the mother's body. Each tsetse fly mother only produces up to 12 offspring in the whole of her lifetime.

LIVE YOUNG

Two female beetles have found comfortable spots on the leaves of a Brazilian rainforest tree and halt for a while. They are an unusual species of leaf beetle and will not lay eggs but give birth to live larvae. Their young have coloring a little lighter than their own, and there are several in each batch. In all, there are approximately 400,000 species of beetle that have been discovered so far, but only a small number reproduce in this way. Many insects abandon their eggs immediately after laying, but live birth means that the young are protected inside the mother until sufficiently well developed to emerge.

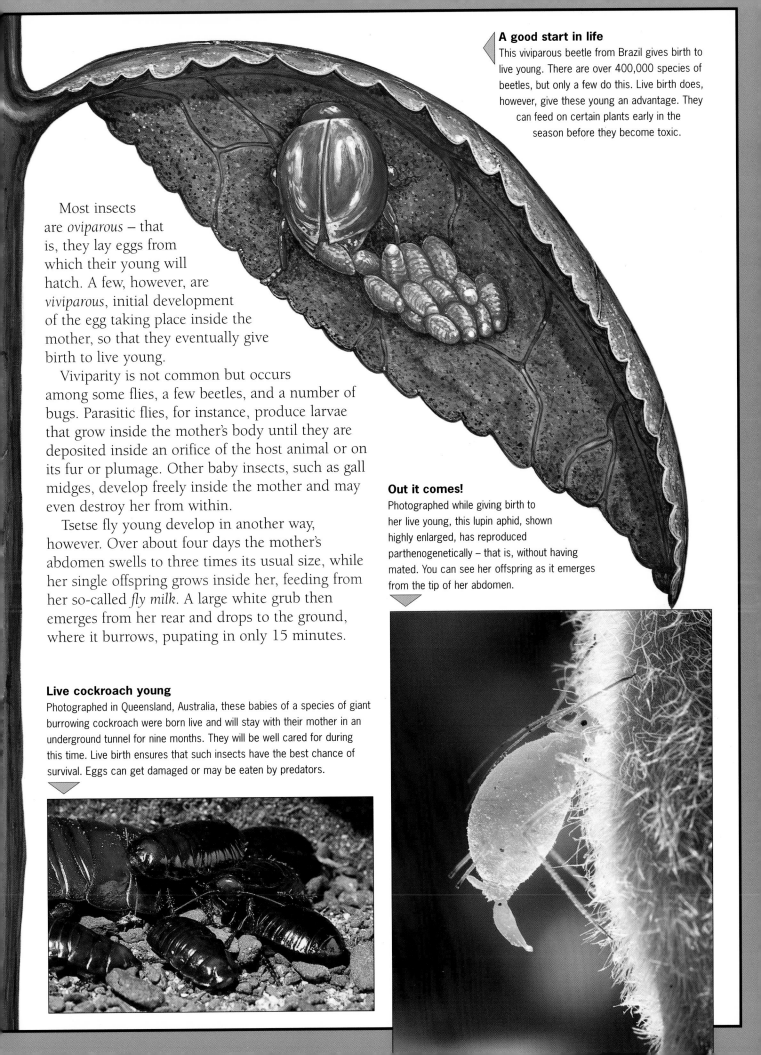

This viviparous beetle from Brazil gives birth to live young. There are over 400,000 species of beetles, but only a few do this. Live birth does, however, give these young an advantage. They can feed on certain plants early in the season before they become toxic.

Most insects are *oviparous* – that is, they lay eggs from which their young will hatch. A few, however, are *viviparous*, initial development of the egg taking place inside the mother, so that they eventually give birth to live young.

Viviparity is not common but occurs among some flies, a few beetles, and a number of bugs. Parasitic flies, for instance, produce larvae that grow inside the mother's body until they are deposited inside an orifice of the host animal or on its fur or plumage. Other baby insects, such as gall midges, develop freely inside the mother and may even destroy her from within.

Tsetse fly young develop in another way, however. Over about four days the mother's abdomen swells to three times its usual size, while her single offspring grows inside her, feeding from her so-called *fly milk*. A large white grub then emerges from her rear and drops to the ground, where it burrows, pupating in only 15 minutes.

Out it comes!

Photographed while giving birth to her live young, this lupin aphid, shown highly enlarged, has reproduced parthenogenetically – that is, without having mated. You can see her offspring as it emerges from the tip of her abdomen.

Live cockroach young

Photographed in Queensland, Australia, these babies of a species of giant burrowing cockroach were born live and will stay with their mother in an underground tunnel for nine months. They will be well cared for during this time. Live birth ensures that such insects have the best chance of survival. Eggs can get damaged or may be eaten by predators.

WITH MATES OR WITHOUT

Some stick insects reproduce when the male and female get together; but from the day that they are born, some females never see a male of their species. Once they are adults, they will feel the urge to reproduce. But without ever having mated, they then start to lay. The eggs will develop normally; and when they hatch, the emerging stick insects may go on to reproduce in exactly the same way. Such insects are *parthenogenetic* – that is, they do not need to mate to produce young.

Producing the next generation

Also known commonly as walking sticks, stick insects vary according to species in the way they reproduce as well as in their shape. Some females do not need to mate with a male to produce fertile eggs, but others reproduce sexually.

All on their own

The masses of lupin aphids in this photograph are all females and can reproduce asexually – that is, parthenogenetically, or without a mate. They do this for several generations all summer. In the fall, however, they give birth to both male and female offspring, all wingless, which mate.

No need for a mate

This swelling on an acorn has been caused by a gall wasp larva. The first generation of oak gall wasps reproduces without the need for a mate and are all females. The second generation are males and females, however, that reproduce sexually.

Several types of aphids are able to reproduce parthinogenetically in warm weather and will multiply rapidly. The females reproduce entirely on their own at this time of the year. But in the autumn aphids usually like to mate, and the females will go on to produce fertilized eggs.

Some queen bees also have an unusual way of reproducing. They store sperm from the drones that have mated with them and then release some, together with an egg, at intervals. If the egg is fertilized, it will produce a female: if not, it will produce a male. This is in fact the only way that males of the species are born.

Some bugs are even *hermaphrodites* and have both male and female reproductive organs, fertilizing themselves when they feel the urge to reproduce. Meanwhile, many of the cells of a single fertilized egg of one type of tiny wasp may each start to develop into a wasp, so that over one thousand are produced from just one egg.

AROUND PEOPLE

Insects are everywhere; and at some point in your life, you are almost certain to fall victim to one, whether it is a cockroach in the kitchen, a wasp on a picnic, or moths in the closet.

In some instances insect infestation spells much more serious dangers, however. Did you know, for instance, that a swarm can contain over 30 billion locusts that will consume more in a day than the whole human population of New York City?

However, most insects are virtually harmless, and some are even highly beneficial – to the extent that without them, life as we know it might simply not exist. There would be no paper to make this book, no fruit or vegetables to eat, and no honey to spread on your muffins. Some are even edible, providing vital sustenance in parts of the world where food is otherwise scarce, or expensive treats for those who appreciate such delicacies as chocolate-covered ants. We invite you now to read on as we put insects under the microscope and examine the way in which these tiny creatures interact with us.

Friends and foes
Bees will often sting; but they also produce honey for us. Open up to other ways in which insects are either useful or harmful to human beings as you look through chapter.

Termite attack
Some termites bite, and all eat at wood, ruining buildings if they have the chance. Some beetles can do a lot of damage, too, as described on pages 158-159.

Poisonous insects
Some insects, such as this beautiful monarch butterfly, contain chemicals that are poisonous. So be sure never to eat an insect unless you are absolutely sure it is harmless and cannot make you ill. Appearances can be deceptive.

Edible bugs
How safe is it to eat some insects? Are they nutritious? How are they cooked? And are they sometimes served in restaurants? On pages 148-149, we give you a taste of several unusual dishes made from a whole variety of creepy-crawlies.

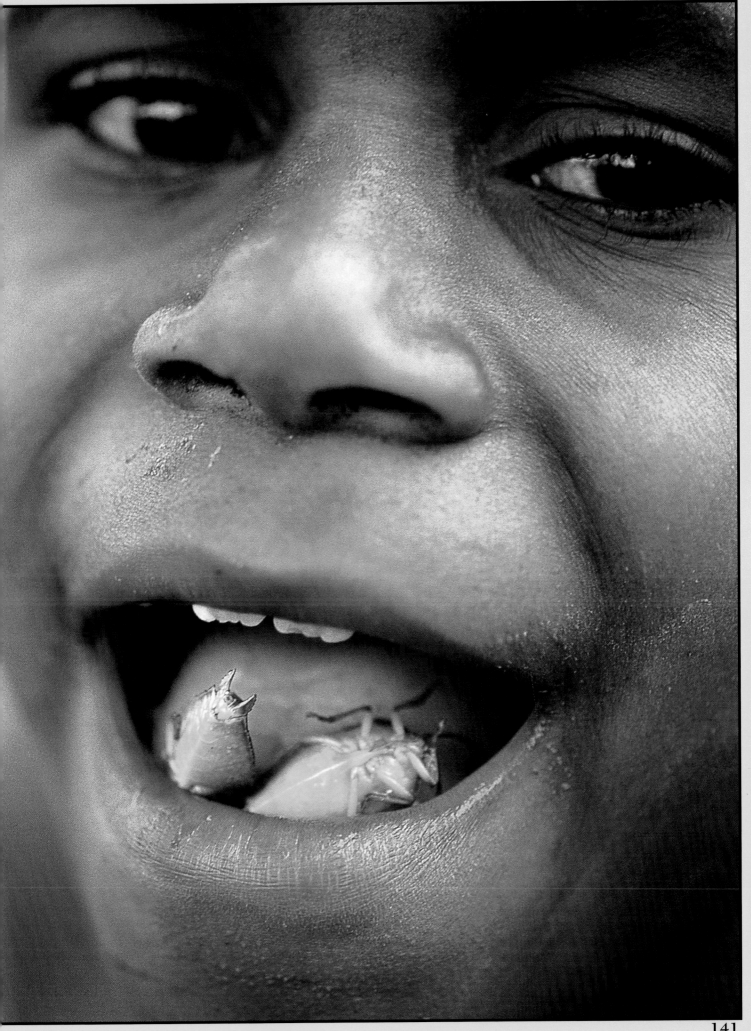

Flying fertilizer

The hoverfly, left, one of over 4,000 known species of this insect, is in the process of visiting a flower. Flowers and many insects live symbiotically. Insects rely on the plants for food in the form of nectar, and the flowers, in return, get the insects to pollinate them.

THE POLLINATORS

Full baskets

When a bee brushes off the pollen that collects on her furry coat as she feeds on a flower's nectar, she packs it into special baskets, visible here as yellow lumps on the outer surfaces of her two back legs. This is a very convenient way of transporting the pollen back to the hive.

Welcome caller

As the fly, above, feeds on nectar, pollen is brushed onto its body. It may transfer it from the male to the female parts of the same plant or to another plant of the same type.

From plant to plant

Ants sometimes climb up stems to seek nectar. As they do this, they get a dusting of pollen and may later transfer pollen to another plant without even being aware of it.

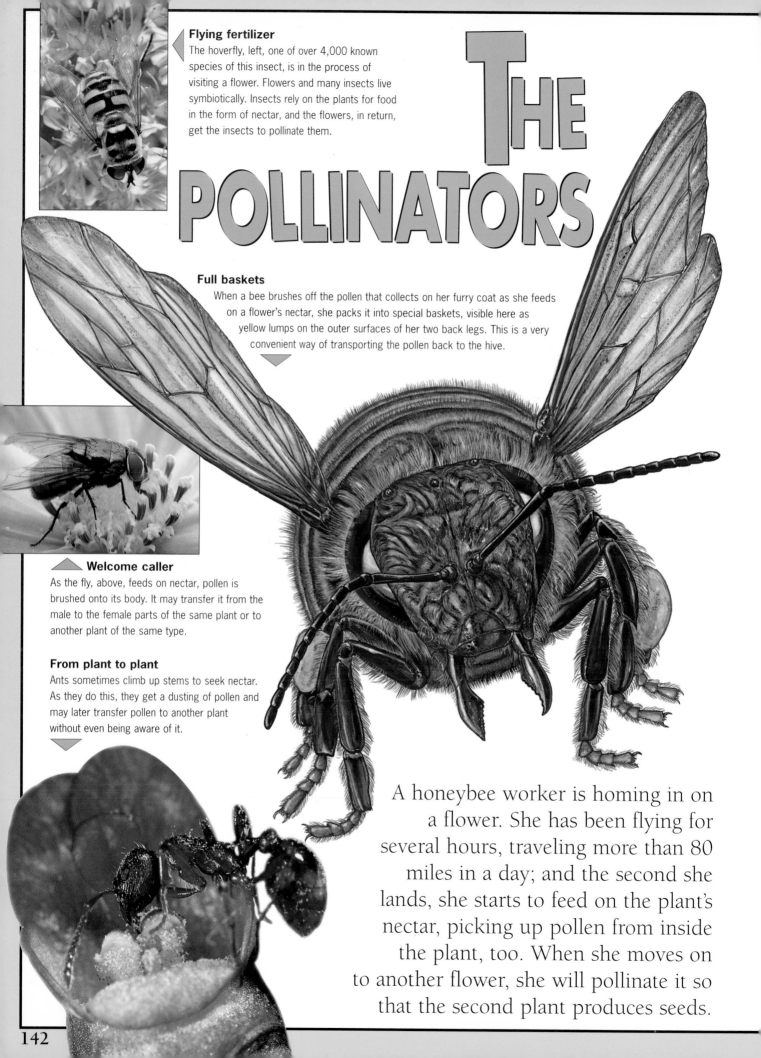

A honeybee worker is homing in on a flower. She has been flying for several hours, traveling more than 80 miles in a day; and the second she lands, she starts to feed on the plant's nectar, picking up pollen from inside the plant, too. When she moves on to another flower, she will pollinate it so that the second plant produces seeds.

Big and smelly

In the rainforest of Sumatra a man stops to admire the world's largest and worst smelling flower, the rafflesia, and holds his breath. Fortunately, greenbottles like its aroma and will pollinate the plant.

Right inside

The vision of insects extends to the ultraviolet spectrum so that they can see color completely invisible to us. Lots of insects, such as the beetle above, are attracted to plants in this way and follow special honey guides that direct them straight to the nectar. In the process they pollinate.

Among the most important of all the insect pollinators are the bees. In total there are over 20,000 species of bees, and all are pollinators to some degree. In fact, without this vast army of pollinators, the growing of crops, such as fruit and some vegetables, as well as flowers, would be impossible. They are usually very furry so that when they visit a flowering plant, pollen grains get stuck to their hairs, only to be brushed off later when they call elsewhere so that pollination occurs.

Some plants are attractive to a wide range of insect-pollinators such as flies, bees, butterflies, or moths, while others are much more specific. The Australian wasp orchid, for example, is only ever pollinated by one species of wasp. Other plants will even entrap their insect-pollinators and not let them go until pollination has taken place.

IN PARALLEL

Flowering plants first appeared during Cretaceous times, around 190 million years ago; and paleobotanists believe that many pollinating insects, such as bees, emerged at around the same time, so that they have evolved in parallel.

Not all plants have visible flowers, yet they still need pollinating. Only the tiny female fig wasp, for instance, can enter the Capri fig's berrylike structure to pollinate the flowers within. Many flies also pollinate plants, including the world's largest flower, the giant rafflesia from Southeast Asia, which grows to over three feet in diameter. Greenbottles cannot resist its disgusting smell.

Oily coatings

Some types of pollen have a coating of oil that will stick to any insect that comes into contact with it. As this wasp does the rounds of some figwort plants, it will inevitably become covered in such grains.

MAKING HONEY

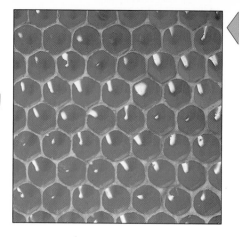

Sweet cells
The central cells of each comb are usually reserved for the eggs, larvae, and pupae. Around them is another ring of cells containing pollen, and beyond this ring are cells in which honey is stored.

Covered from head to toe in special clothing, a beekeeper inspects the honeycombs in one of her hives. If the bees suddenly become more active, she will use a strange-looking device called a smoker to puff smoke onto the combs. Once the bees start to suck up honey – their main source of nourishment in the hive – and have full stomachs, they will become less aggressive and leave the beekeeper to carry on with her work.

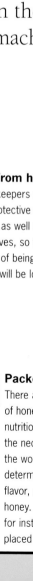

From head to toe
Beekeepers need to wear special protective clothing and helmets, as well as heavy-duty gloves, so that the risk of being stung repeatedly will be lowered.

Packed with goodness
There are thousands of types of honey, and all are highly nutritious. The source of the nectar collected by the worker bees determines the color, flavor, and aroma of the honey. Orange-blossom honey, for instance, comes from hives placed in orange orchards.

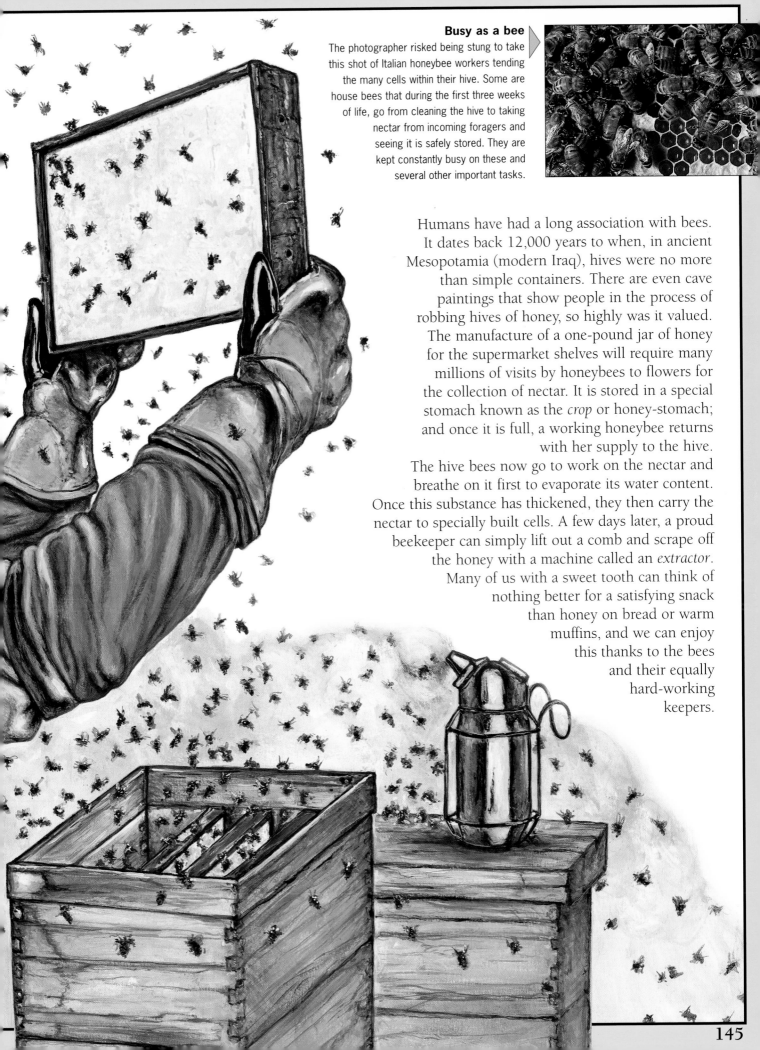

Humans have had a long association with bees. It dates back 12,000 years to when, in ancient Mesopotamia (modern Iraq), hives were no more than simple containers. There are even cave paintings that show people in the process of robbing hives of honey, so highly was it valued. The manufacture of a one-pound jar of honey for the supermarket shelves will require many millions of visits by honeybees to flowers for the collection of nectar. It is stored in a special stomach known as the *crop* or honey-stomach; and once it is full, a working honeybee returns with her supply to the hive.

The hive bees now go to work on the nectar and breathe on it first to evaporate its water content. Once this substance has thickened, they then carry the nectar to specially built cells. A few days later, a proud beekeeper can simply lift out a comb and scrape off the honey with a machine called an *extractor*. Many of us with a sweet tooth can think of nothing better for a satisfying snack than honey on bread or warm muffins, and we can enjoy this thanks to the bees and their equally hard-working keepers.

After eating its fill of mulberry leaves, a fully-grown silkworm prepares to make the last journey of its life. Years of breeding by humans have left it with weak legs, and this makes walking, climbing, and any attempt at escaping very difficult. Slowly, however, the caterpillar hauls its body up the bamboo structure provided for its pupation. Once it has spun its cocoon, it will be killed so that the threads it exudes can be used in the manufacture of silk.

One of the most precious materials in the ancient world was silk, and for thousands of years the only country to produce it in any quantity was China. Over 4,000 years ago a Chinese princess called Hsi Ling-Shi helped develop the art of silk-making. A special moth was found to produce fine silk and kept in captivity. Its ability to fly was bred out to make the moth easier to control. It was, entomologists think, the first domesticated insect.

For many hundreds of years the Chinese guarded the secrets of its manufacture jealously. Anybody caught trying to smuggle the formula to another country was executed. It was only a matter of time, however, before two monks got both eggs and pupae out of China, bringing them to Emperor Justinian 1 in Constantinople (now Istanbul in Turkey.)

Today silk is produced in various parts of the world, including Vietnam, Thailand, Japan, and Italy, although most of the world's supply still comes from China. To make an average-sized silk sleeveless dress, nearly 2,000 cocoons are required, while about 300 may be needed for a necktie. Although it is undoubtedly a beautiful fabric, many people will not wear silk out of respect for the thousands of silkworms that never had the chance of maturing into adult moths.

Out of the East

This detail from an old Chinese print shows silkworms being fed as part of the silk production process. For centuries the secret of silk-making was closely guarded by the imperial family, and it remains an important industry in China today, as well as in Thailand, Japan, and Vietnam.

Spinning away

Seen in closeup, the Chinese silk moth larva, above, is spinning its cocoon before pupating. Astonishingly, in spite of its small size, it can spin at a rate of about 6 inches per minute, and a single strand may be as long as half a mile.

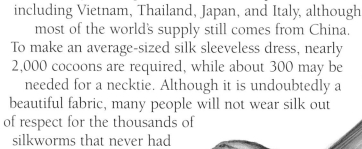

Factory farming

Thousands of silkworms work at spinning their cocoons on a silk farm in Vietnam, left. The fabric for which they give their lives is warm in winter, cool in summer, shiny, lightweight, strong, and highly commercial.

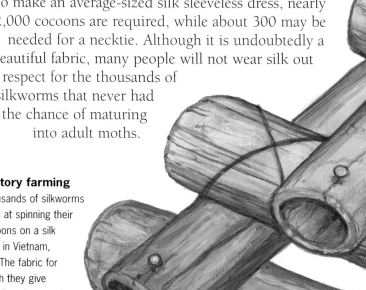

THE STORY OF SILK

Brief lives

Silk moth caterpillars are gathered and placed separately within racks. They are then left to spin. When the cocoons are ready, they are removed and placed in boiling water. The pupae inside the cocoons are killed off in this way. The outer layer of the silken thread is then removed so that it takes on a glossy appearance. The silk from several thousands of cocoons is then wound onto spools ready for soaking, dyeing, and weaving.

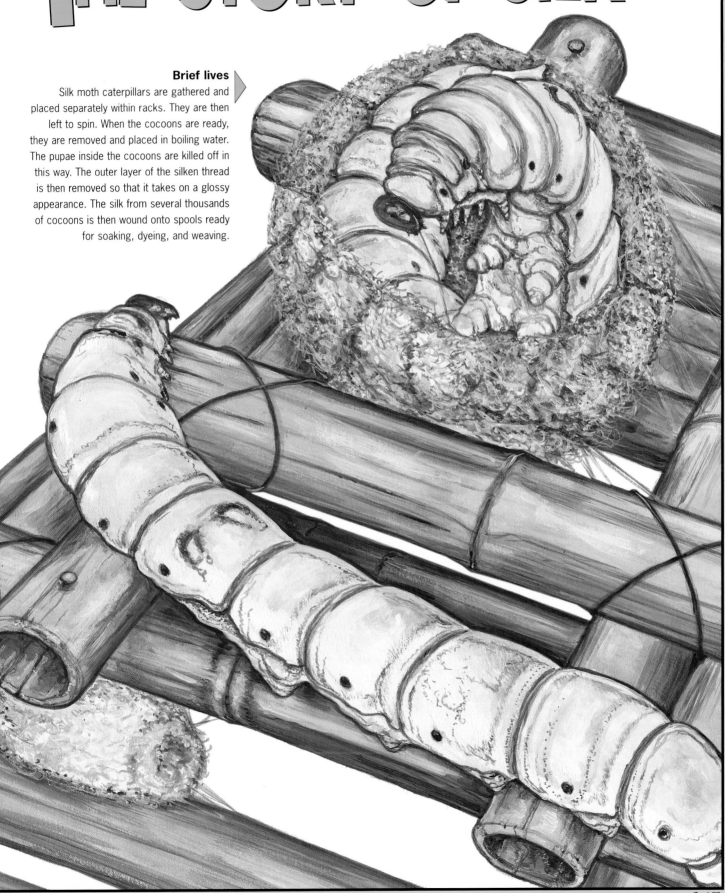

What's cooking?
You might not have guessed, but this mouth-watering meal, photographed in China, contains fried silkworm pupae, believed to have health-giving properties.

Strange treat
Perhaps you often enjoy a meal of pasta. Would you find it so appetizing, however, if you saw it listed on a Mexican menu as mealworm spaghetti?

Tasty grubs
For some peoples of the world both grubs and mature insects form a major part of the daily diet and provide valuable calories. In fact, a whole plateful may be even more nutritious than a pizza.

EDIBLE INSECTS

In the Australian outback an Aborigine uses a thin knife to whittle away at a tree stump until he exposes an insect larva. He pops it in his mouth. It is nutritious and very tasty.

Lots of us, particularly in the West, have taboos about eating insects. Scientists consider, however, that we could be missing a cheap and healthy addition to our diet. In fact, more than 500 species of insect are eaten regularly worldwide. They are low in fat and, pound for pound, are much higher in protein than red meat, poultry, or fish. They can also be reared in large numbers without the cruelty associated with other forms of livestock farming. In China experiments have even begun in producing food from pulverized maggots. Be warned, though: it would be extremely unwise to try eating an insect unless you know for certain it is not poisonous and will taste delicious if cooked properly.

An unusual meal

The table is set most elegantly at a very expensive restaurant in the Far East, and the tourists are eager to try the local fare. Fried giant water bugs feature on the menu as dish of the day. Will they dare to sample it? They have never tasted water bugs before and are wary.

Cicadas for supper

Among the many unusual foods to be found in the markets of Cambodia are cooked cicadas. This dish was once popular in Greece, too, and is mentioned in the writings of the great philosopher Aristotle. He said that the nymphs and males tasted best.

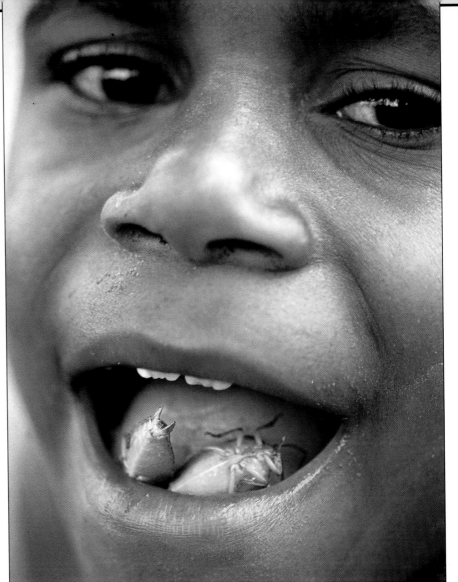

Snacking on a stink bug

This boy from a forest village in the heart of Indonesia loves to snack on roasted stink bugs and proves it for the photographer. Other insects are eaten in this island nation, as are some spiders.

Stir-fried ants

Cambodians regard ants as a delicacy and sometimes serve them with rice and vegetables. In some parts of Africa, meanwhile, long-bodied ants, known as Bushman's rice, are eaten. Termites, too, are eaten there. But of course, those who eat insects must be able to distinguish the poisonous from the edible.

149

HELP IN THE GARDEN

Artful ants
Ants can be beneficial to the soil and are useful scavengers. Yet in one particular way they may be the bane of a gardener's life. As you can see in the photograph shown above, they will milk and tend the much-hated aphids, while the aphids suck the plants dry.

It is late spring, and the garden is already full of activity. Caterpillars are chewing their way through leaves, while aphids suck sap from prize rose bushes. Elsewhere, numerous other insects are rapidly consuming vegetation, too. But they do not have it all their own way. An army of bright red, black-spotted beetles is preparing to do battle with these pests and descends on a shrub. In no time, scores of these ladybugs start to feed on the aphids and caterpillars. Come summer, the garden will look its best after all.

Young assistance
A seven-spot ladybug pupa lengthens as the adult form is about to emerge. It will soon be feeding on aphids, much to the gardener's delight.

Pest control
Wasps not only pollinate flowers but also earn their keep by feeding themselves and their young on the larvae of insects that are dreadful plant pests. In the fall they have the reward of fruit instead of nectar.

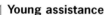

Three cheers for ladybugs!
As soon as a ladybug larva hatches, it is able to munch its way through up to 30 aphids every day. The seven-spot ladybug also likes to feed on the larvae of the dreaded Colorado beetle. People with vegetable gardens – and farmers, too – often make the effort to bring in lots of ladbugs as natural pest-controllers for their potato plants.

Perhaps you think of a flower garden as a place just for plants. It will also be home, however, to hundreds of different species of insects. A great many of them will be pests, but they only become a real nuisance if there are not enough predators to keep their numbers down. This way of dealing with unwanted insects is much better than wide use of insecticides; for although there are some chemicals that will target specific species, most kill a wide range of both harmful and helpful insects. Even those chemicals that only destroy one type of insect will have the effect of forcing a natural and therefore very welcome predator to go elsewhere to look for food. Encouraging insects that are actively good for your plants – ladybugs and bees, for instance – into the garden is definitely sound planting practice.

LENDING A HAND

Wasps, too, are welcome visitors to a garden, in spite of their reputation as stinging insects. In fact, they are vital allies in the fight against pests, particularly during the early part of the year when many pest-insects are going through their main feeding stage. Only later in the year does taste move from the diet provided by garden pests to more sugary substances. Lots of other soil-dwelling insects, meanwhile, help keep the earth in good condition. In fact, without the help of insects, most gardens would definitely fail to bloom and revert to being no more than an uninteresting bare patch.

Mealtime
This ladybug larva, shown at 15 times its natural size in a photomicrograph, is busy feeding on an aphid, its favorite meal. Ladybug larvae feed constantly for about three weeks before pupating. As adults, too, they continue to feed on aphids. The two insects in this image have been artificially colored for easy recognition.

PLAGUES OF LOCUSTS

Edible swarms
Farmers have had to contend with locusts since biblical times, but some species have always been eaten in a few parts of the world. Even the strict Jewish dietary laws allow some types of locust to be eaten.

Desert species
Only by eating continuously do desert locusts manage to survive in very hot, dry climates. At the nymph stage, as shown in this photograph, they have only stumps for wings but will be able to fly in swarms containing billions of their kind after several molts.

What an appetite!
This young locust is one of several species that undertake mass migrations, forming enormous swarms and devastating all of the vegetation in their path. It is seen here at three times its actual size.

With a loud flapping of wings, a cloud of locusts descends, and the newly ripened crop disappears rapidly between the clicking jaws of these ever-hungry insects. Angry, the farmer starts to wave a stick in an attempt to scare them away, but they are not stopped. Within the hour the whole field has been laid bare. However, all is not lost. Patiently, he gathers up great handfuls of the locusts and stuffs them into a sack. He is taking them home to provide food for his family.

Keeping them at bay
In remote regions, it is sometimes left to an individual farmer to cope with a locust swarm. However, these insects do not respect borders. The problem therefore becomes an international one, which is why the United Nations Food and Agricultural Organization now has an emergency center that warns about invading locust swarms.

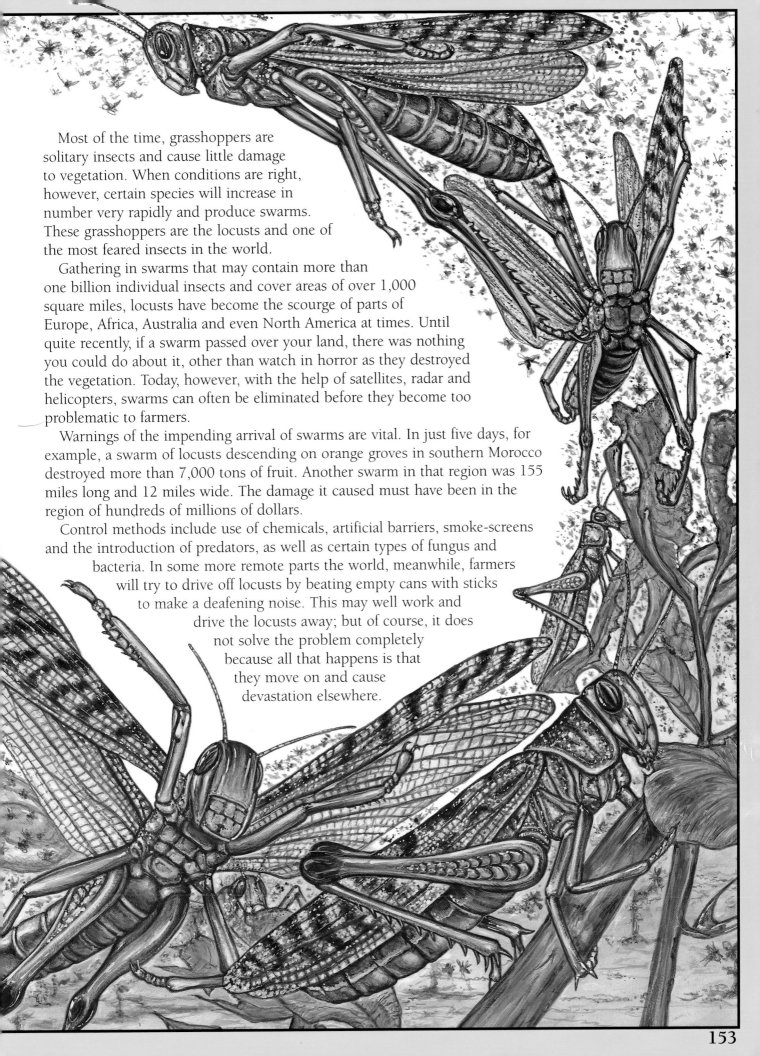

Most of the time, grasshoppers are solitary insects and cause little damage to vegetation. When conditions are right, however, certain species will increase in number very rapidly and produce swarms. These grasshoppers are the locusts and one of the most feared insects in the world.

Gathering in swarms that may contain more than one billion individual insects and cover areas of over 1,000 square miles, locusts have become the scourge of parts of Europe, Africa, Australia and even North America at times. Until quite recently, if a swarm passed over your land, there was nothing you could do about it, other than watch in horror as they destroyed the vegetation. Today, however, with the help of satellites, radar and helicopters, swarms can often be eliminated before they become too problematic to farmers.

Warnings of the impending arrival of swarms are vital. In just five days, for example, a swarm of locusts descending on orange groves in southern Morocco destroyed more than 7,000 tons of fruit. Another swarm in that region was 155 miles long and 12 miles wide. The damage it caused must have been in the region of hundreds of millions of dollars.

Control methods include use of chemicals, artificial barriers, smoke-screens and the introduction of predators, as well as certain types of fungus and bacteria. In some more remote parts the world, meanwhile, farmers will try to drive off locusts by beating empty cans with sticks to make a deafening noise. This may well work and drive the locusts away; but of course, it does not solve the problem completely because all that happens is that they move on and cause devastation elsewhere.

GETTING STUNG

Foraging for food in a forest clearing, a female giant ant stops to taste the air and recognizes at once that nearby there is something that is sweet. Speeding up, the ant scurries off in the direction of the aroma. Soon, she arrives at a human finger on which there are traces of jello. The ant has stumbled on a picnic site. Just as she starts to feed, however, she senses danger. Her response is to twist her abdomen around very quickly and then bury her long stinger into the flesh. Her powerful abdomen muscles now force venom along the hollow stinger and into the victim. Not all ants sting, but this species does. Ouch!

Painful encounters
Some ants use stingers, and others spray formic acid as a form of self-defense. Either will have an unpleasant effect on a human and may be deadly or crippling to an insect enemy. Some venoms contain histamine, which may cause a particularly bad reaction. Prompt medical attention will be required.

Little nippers
Australian weaver ants may be small and innocent-looking; but as shown in this photograph, they can pack a nasty bite and will also squirt acid from the end of their abdomen. Their jaws are remarkably strong, and an attack such as this will certainly be very painful to an unfortunate victim.

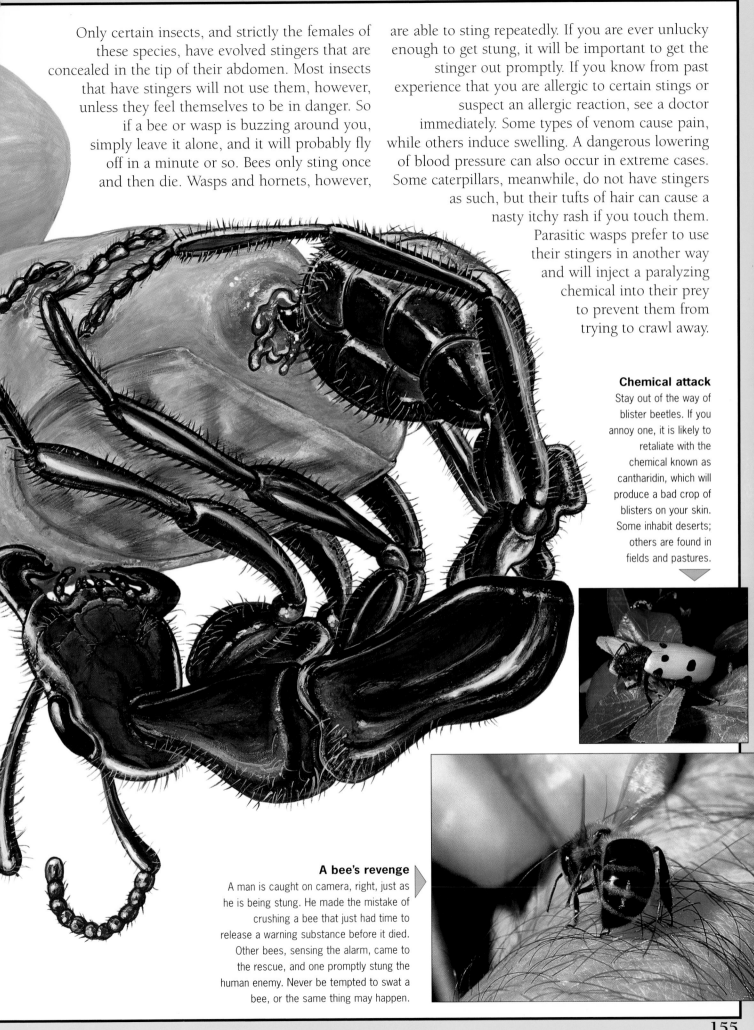

Only certain insects, and strictly the females of these species, have evolved stingers that are concealed in the tip of their abdomen. Most insects that have stingers will not use them, however, unless they feel themselves to be in danger. So if a bee or wasp is buzzing around you, simply leave it alone, and it will probably fly off in a minute or so. Bees only sting once and then die. Wasps and hornets, however, are able to sting repeatedly. If you are ever unlucky enough to get stung, it will be important to get the stinger out promptly. If you know from past experience that you are allergic to certain stings or suspect an allergic reaction, see a doctor immediately. Some types of venom cause pain, while others induce swelling. A dangerous lowering of blood pressure can also occur in extreme cases. Some caterpillars, meanwhile, do not have stingers as such, but their tufts of hair can cause a nasty itchy rash if you touch them. Parasitic wasps prefer to use their stingers in another way and will inject a paralyzing chemical into their prey to prevent them from trying to crawl away.

Chemical attack
Stay out of the way of blister beetles. If you annoy one, it is likely to retaliate with the chemical known as cantharidin, which will produce a bad crop of blisters on your skin. Some inhabit deserts; others are found in fields and pastures.

A bee's revenge
A man is caught on camera, right, just as he is being stung. He made the mistake of crushing a bee that just had time to release a warning substance before it died. Other bees, sensing the alarm, came to the rescue, and one promptly stung the human enemy. Never be tempted to swat a bee, or the same thing may happen.

155

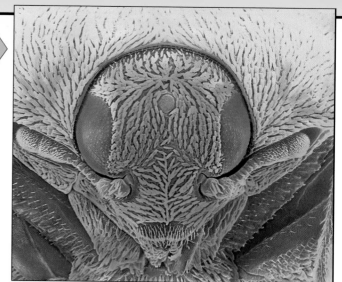

Frantic feeders
High magnification and use of false coloring clearly reveal the structure of a carpet beetle's head. Its larvae are serious pests. Able to digest keratin, they love to eat away at hair and wool, and even feathers. If they get into the pile of a rug, there will soon be lots of bare patches.

CHAMPION CHEWERS

Carpet-crawlers
Furs, fabrics, and stored food may all be damaged by the larvae of the carpet beetle, shown in the photograph above. They have the most enormous appetites.

In the dark and warmth of a centrally heated apartment in New York, caterpillars of the clothes moth have been hard at work all through the winter. To them the tough, dry fibers that were knitted together to make a sweater for Alice were delicious; and this once delightful garment is now spotted with tiny holes. Suddenly the closet door opens, and light floods in. As Alice comes to look for something to wear, she notices the damage. Mature moths that are nestling in the wardrobe quickly scuttle into the shadows.

In the dark
Clothes moths far prefer to spend time huddling in the dark and, if disturbed, will usually head for a corner rather than flying out of a window.

Clothes moths are tiny, with a wingspan measuring about half an inch. Pale in color, they often have a slight golden hue to their wings. Who would have thought that such small, innocent-looking creatures could be such wanton vandals at an early stage in their lives! They are most often found indoors where their larvae feed on the fabric of clothes, carpets, and sometimes mattresses, too. Adult moths are not responsible for such damage, however, since they do not feed beyond the caterpillar stage and are very short-lived.

Caterpillars of the clothes moth weave silken cocoons that may be covered with fibers taken from wool. Fortunately, however, they are no longer the very widespread pests that they once were due to the fact that we are now so much more careful about the regular washing of our garments or have our clothes dry-cleaned. These processes will eliminate clothes moth larvae for the most part.

A ruined collection

It is not only clothes and furnishings that insects will attack. Even a butterfly collection can be destroyed by the larvae of greedy beetles that somehow get into a display case like the one shown here.

Closet invaders

If you spot moths that have somehow got into your closet, try to get rid of them before they have a chance to lay more eggs. If they hatch, the emerging larvae will no doubt do major damage to lots of garments, including hats and even your sneakers.

157

BEETLE DAMAGE

A male deathwatch beetle is crawling along the rafters of an old house. It is nearly midnight, and all is quiet – until, that is, the beetle begins to bang his head against the hard surface of the wood. The purpose of this endless rapping is to attract a mate. A female will eventually hear the call and seek him out.

Infestation

Woodworm and deathwatch beetle damage is more common in old houses. This may be because timber for furniture or beams was formerly kept outdoors and allowed to season prior to use. During this time, initial infestation may have occurred.

Exit holes

This furniture beetle has just emerged from one of its holes in a piece of plywood. The timber is now unsuitable for use, although the "distressed" look is often a feature of faked antiques.

An adult woodworm beetle will bore into wood and lay its eggs in any small crevice. However, if furniture is kept highly polished, there is less risk of infestation.

The evidence
Much of this very old table has been literally turned to dust as a result of woodworm. The many holes provide evidence of the presence of these vandals.

Deathwatch beetles have no respect for the fabric of a house; and although less familiar today because of the use of modern materials and preventive chemicals, they are still to be found in old buildings. Naturally, their ability to turn wood into dust does not make them the most popular of guests. In the wild these beetles play a vital role in the breaking down of dead wood. But once they manage to come indoors, they still have the urge to complete their lifecycle, and it is their larvae that do the damage. As soon as they hatch, they start to bore into furniture, floorboards, or wooden paneling – anywhere, in fact, that the eggs happen to have been laid; and they may remain there for several years before pupating. When the adult beetle is ready to emerge, it gnaws its way out of the wood, leaving a small, round exit hole – a sure sign that the wood has been infested.

Knocking on wood
If you ever hear repeated knocking sounds coming from a piece of wooden furniture, it is probably deathwatch beetles calling to find a mate. Deep inside, they will be tapping with their heads against the surface on which they are standing. The noise that they make sounds like a monotonous, dull thud.

THE UNWELCOME ROACH

Horrible habits

The American cockroach, originally from Florida but now found in many parts of the world outside the United States, likes nothing better than to vomit its stomach contents and to defecate on your food. Keep them out of your home!

Bug alert!

Cockroaches have been known to get into all sorts of kitchen equipment. Toasters, microwave ovens, blenders, lighting, food-mixers – all have been invaded by cockroaches at times. They have even crawled into computers and could do damage to wiring if they start to chew at it.

It is warm and free from predators inside the computer, and therefore an ideal place for cockroaches to set up home. But Daryl cannot believe his eyes as he peeks in and sees them. There are several that have died inside the computer. Here their bodies dried out quickly, which is why their antennae became curled instead of straight.

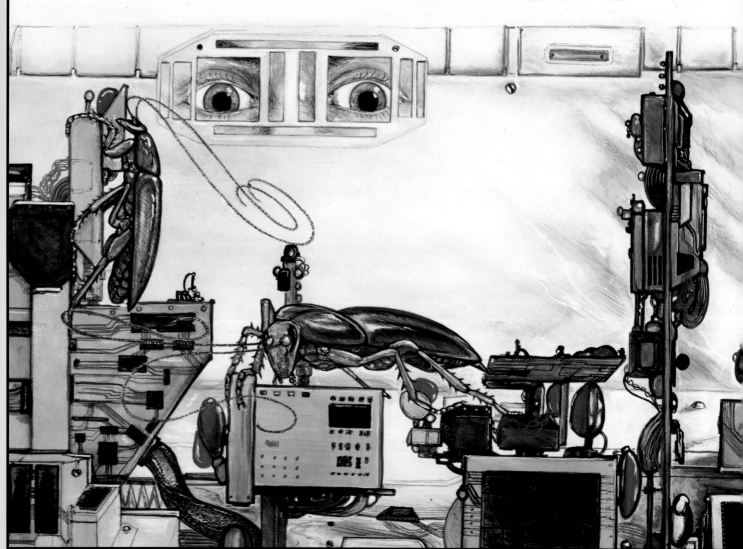

In the wild many species of cockroaches are to be found between rocks, inside caves, or among leaf-litter on a forest floor. But for some of them, there could be no better place than inside a building. Here, they can roam about equally freely when everyone is asleep in bed.

However, humans have a far from perfect relationship with these pests; for while some are no more than a nuisance, others may be carriers of potentially deadly disease. They will feed on a wide variety of foodstuffs – maybe excrement one moment and crumbs from a sandwich the next. Add to this their obnoxious habit of regurgitating their stomach contents and defecating where they feed, and their potential as germ-spreaders is obvious. In fact, in tropical countries infection spread by cockroaches probably accounts for more infant deaths each year through diarrhea than malaria.

Trying to eradicate cockroaches from the home is no easy task, however. Tough egg sacs protect the young from chemicals, and they can survive long periods of cold. The combination of long antennae, good eyesight, and two highly sensitive projections called *cerci* at their rear also makes them difficult to catch.

Keep it under wraps
If a cockroach finds cookie crumbs on the floor overnight, it will be able to feast. If anyone is then silly enough to eat the cockroach's leftovers the following morning, terrible food-poisoning could result. The cockroach is known to be one of the worst contaminators of the entire insect kingdom.

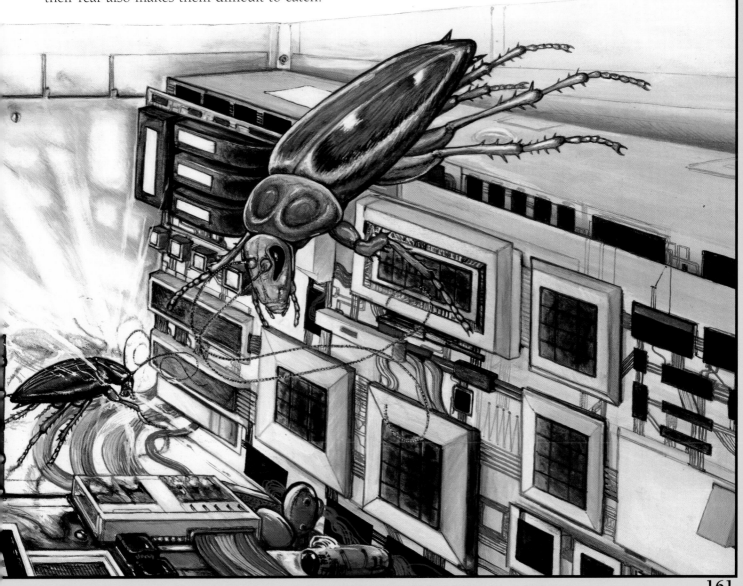

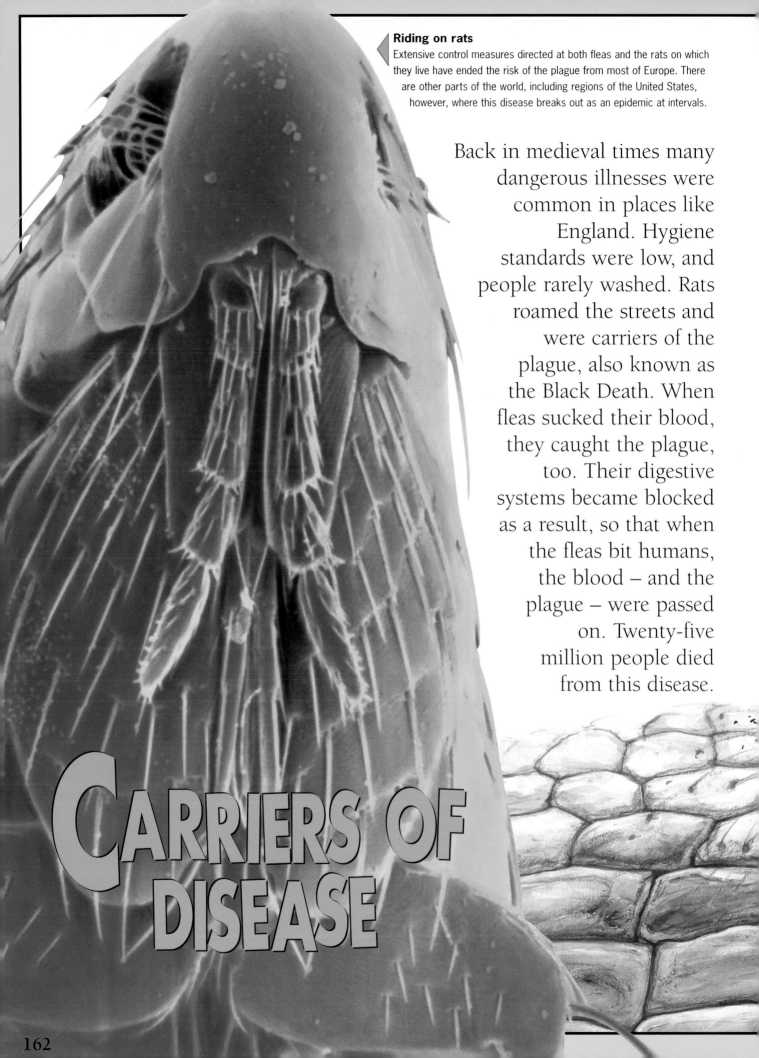

Back in medieval times many dangerous illnesses were common in places like England. Hygiene standards were low, and people rarely washed. Rats roamed the streets and were carriers of the plague, also known as the Black Death. When fleas sucked their blood, they caught the plague, too. Their digestive systems became blocked as a result, so that when the fleas bit humans, the blood – and the plague – were passed on. Twenty-five million people died from this disease.

CARRIERS OF DISEASE

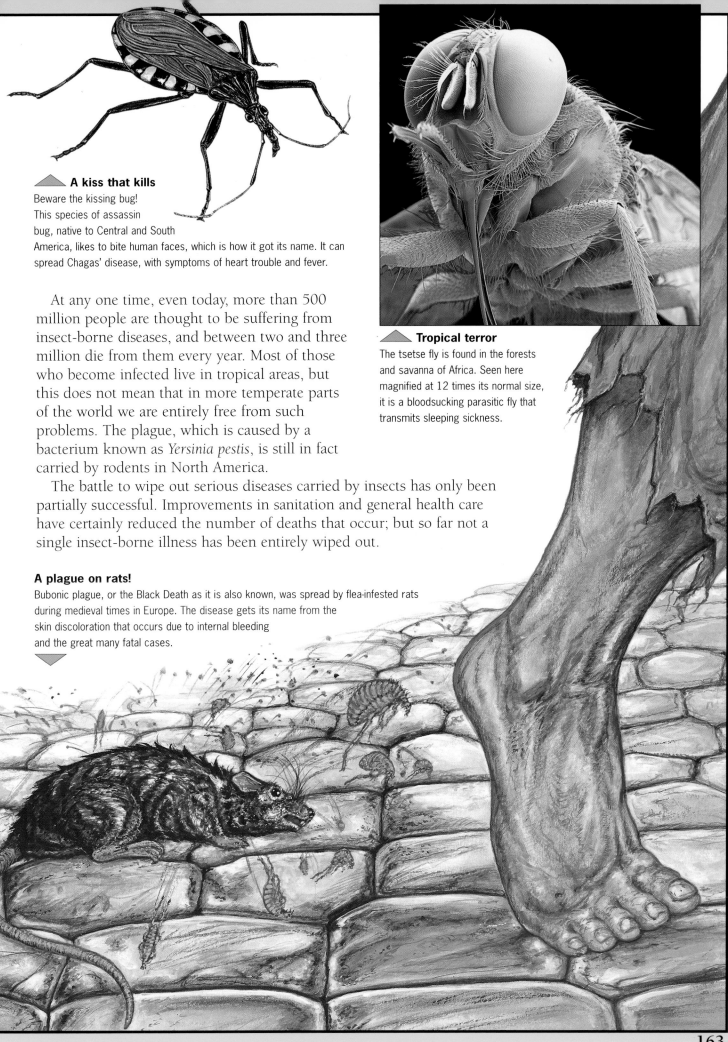

A kiss that kills

Beware the kissing bug! This species of assassin bug, native to Central and South America, likes to bite human faces, which is how it got its name. It can spread Chagas' disease, with symptoms of heart trouble and fever.

At any one time, even today, more than 500 million people are thought to be suffering from insect-borne diseases, and between two and three million die from them every year. Most of those who become infected live in tropical areas, but this does not mean that in more temperate parts of the world we are entirely free from such problems. The plague, which is caused by a bacterium known as *Yersinia pestis*, is still in fact carried by rodents in North America.

The battle to wipe out serious diseases carried by insects has only been partially successful. Improvements in sanitation and general health care have certainly reduced the number of deaths that occur; but so far not a single insect-borne illness has been entirely wiped out.

Tropical terror

The tsetse fly is found in the forests and savanna of Africa. Seen here magnified at 12 times its normal size, it is a bloodsucking parasitic fly that transmits sleeping sickness.

A plague on rats!

Bubonic plague, or the Black Death as it is also known, was spread by flea-infested rats during medieval times in Europe. The disease gets its name from the skin discoloration that occurs due to internal bleeding and the great many fatal cases.

RECORD-BREAKERS

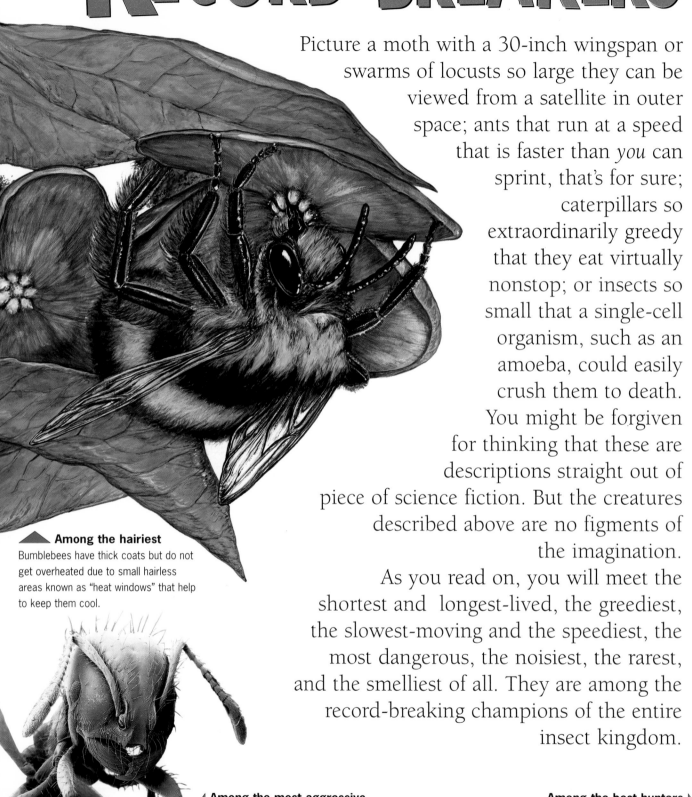

Picture a moth with a 30-inch wingspan or swarms of locusts so large they can be viewed from a satellite in outer space; ants that run at a speed that is faster than *you* can sprint, that's for sure; caterpillars so extraordinarily greedy that they eat virtually nonstop; or insects so small that a single-cell organism, such as an amoeba, could easily crush them to death. You might be forgiven for thinking that these are descriptions straight out of piece of science fiction. But the creatures described above are no figments of the imagination.

As you read on, you will meet the shortest and longest-lived, the greediest, the slowest-moving and the speediest, the most dangerous, the noisiest, the rarest, and the smelliest of all. They are among the record-breaking champions of the entire insect kingdom.

Among the hairiest
Bumblebees have thick coats but do not get overheated due to small hairless areas known as "heat windows" that help to keep them cool.

Among the most aggressive
Tropical fire ants, like the one shown here, may sting painfully if they are disturbed, and swarms of them can even attack and kill small animals.

Among the best hunters
With its grasshopper prey clasped in its forelegs, a praying mantis, one of the insect world's most successful predators, makes a meal of its victim's head.

THE BIGGEST

You might be inclined to dismiss a moth as a small insect no bigger than a housefly. But there is in fact one with a wingspan as wide as from your elbow to the tip of your little finger! The atlas moth is one of the largest known moths, and it is found mainly in the tropical jungle of Sri Lanka and Malaysia. Its extensive wings are richly patterned in many tones of brown. Only the South American giant Agrippa moth rivals it for size. It is hard to believe that the atlas moth was once a small, pale, yellowish-green caterpillar only four inches long with a row of spines all along its back. In both sexes the antennae are heavily feathered, while the forewings have an unusual shape. The sight of it fluttering through the air in the middle of a rainforest environment must be quite scary.

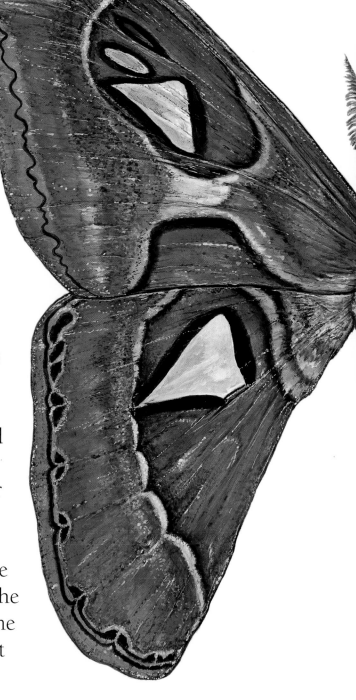

Giant cockroaches

Enormous in comparison with other species of cockroach, this giant is from Trinidad in the West Indies. Like all other insects, however, it will never grow to a monstrous size because of its body structure and the breathing organs that it has. Insects have no internal skeleton to support them, and no lungs either, just simple breathing holes. This form of respiration is not adequate for the needs of a large creature. So you will never find an insect that is larger than a few inches at the most.

Massive moth

You will only come across the atlas moth in its natural enviroment in the rainforests of Asia. If the only moths you have ever seen are tiny clothes moths, you would be astonished by the size of this record-breaker.

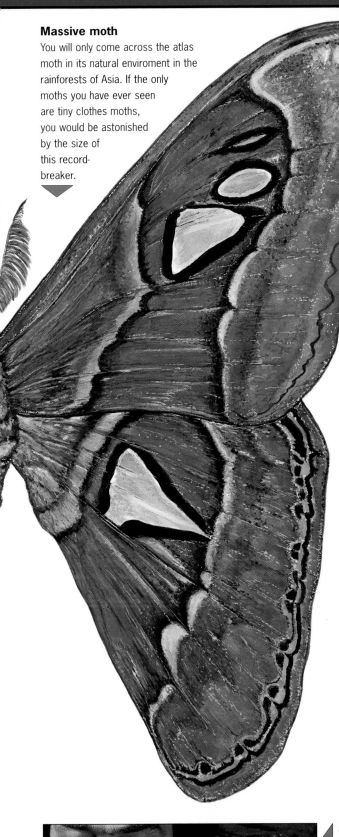

What a whopper!

The Goliath beetle in this photograph comes from Rwanda in Africa and is named after the biblical giant. The males of this species can weigh as much as 3.5 ounces, and their larvae grow to be big, too.

Among the giants of the insect kingdom are a damselfly from South America with a wingspan of over seven inches and a huge stick insect from Indonesia measuring 12 inches in length. The titan longhorn beetle from the Brazilian rainforest is almost the same size but far more fearsome in appearance. The Queen Alexandra's birdwing butterfly from Papua New Guinea has a massive 11-inch wingspan. It is the largest of all the butterflies and now very rare, so that it is listed as an endangered species and protected by international law. You will find pictures of it on page 175. Within each order of insects there may be considerable variation in size; but among the ants, termites, wasps, and bees it is always the queens that are the largest. Prehistoric relatives of dragonflies were far larger than those we know today. Fossilized remains even show them to have been about six times the size. No one knows for sure, however, why these giant insects died out.

Giant wasp

The hornet below is the largest type of wasp found in England. It looks fierce but will not use its stinger unless provoked. Its venom contains a highly toxic cocktail that may kill a hypersensitive victim if the hornet stings, or if the venom gets into a blood vessel.

A huge wingspan

This giant Agrippa moth, photographed sitting like a parrot on a man's shoulder, has the largest wingspan of any known moth – up to 12 inches – and is found in South America. How frightening it must be to come across one at night!

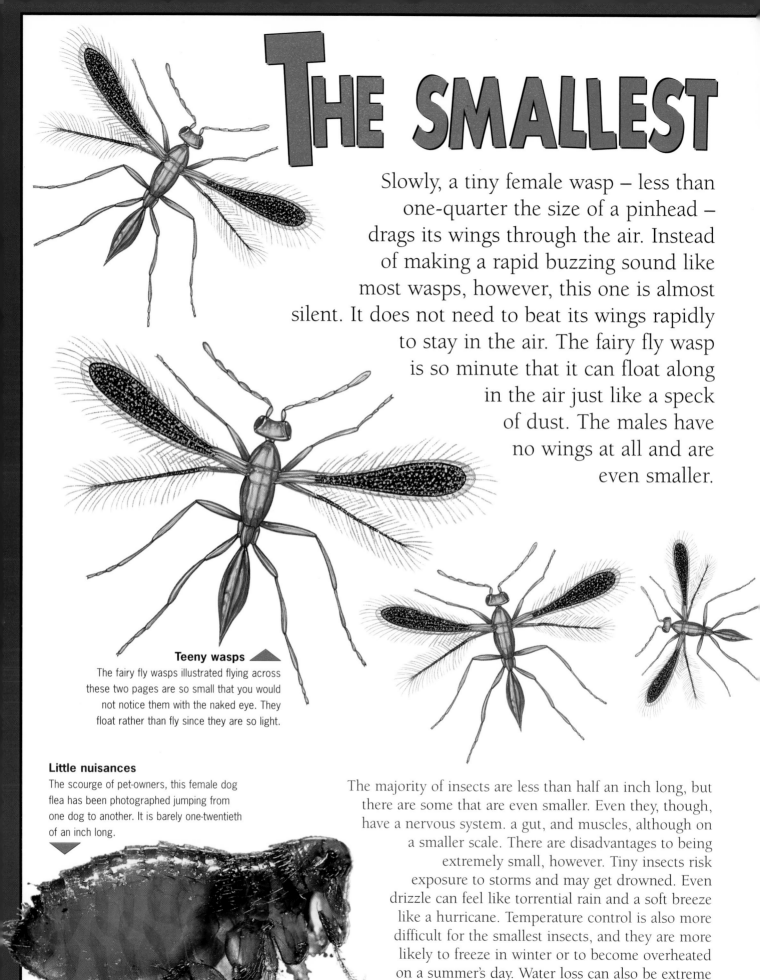

THE SMALLEST

Slowly, a tiny female wasp – less than one-quarter the size of a pinhead – drags its wings through the air. Instead of making a rapid buzzing sound like most wasps, however, this one is almost silent. It does not need to beat its wings rapidly to stay in the air. The fairy fly wasp is so minute that it can float along in the air just like a speck of dust. The males have no wings at all and are even smaller.

Teeny wasps
The fairy fly wasps illustrated flying across these two pages are so small that you would not notice them with the naked eye. They float rather than fly since they are so light.

Little nuisances
The scourge of pet-owners, this female dog flea has been photographed jumping from one dog to another. It is barely one-twentieth of an inch long.

The majority of insects are less than half an inch long, but there are some that are even smaller. Even they, though, have a nervous system. a gut, and muscles, although on a smaller scale. There are disadvantages to being extremely small, however. Tiny insects risk exposure to storms and may get drowned. Even drizzle can feel like torrential rain and a soft breeze like a hurricane. Temperature control is also more difficult for the smallest insects, and they are more likely to freeze in winter or to become overheated on a summer's day. Water loss can also be extreme in the heat unless there is special exoskeletal adaptation to cut it down.

Special entry

These developing fig wasps are so small that when the females eventually mature, they may pollinate certain other types of fig that other insects cannot pollinate because the opening to the plant is too tiny.

Small talk

This tiny mutant fruitfly, shown highly enlarged under the microscope, has been crossbred for genetic experiments.

You might expect the tiniest insects to be harmless, but that is not the case. Some species of fruitflies, for example, are very small – only one-eighth of an inch long – but in spite of their size, they can do a lot of damage as larvae when they feed on flowers or fruit, or form galls. Fleas, lice, and mosquitoes are very small, too, and will bite us at every opportunity.

Other tiny insects are very useful, though. The only entrance to the reproductive parts of the delicious Smyrna fig plant, for example, is a small opening at the top, which bees cannot possibly get into. It is not possible for this plant's pollen to be carried by the wind either, because it is so deep within the plant. What is more, the Smyrna fig only produces female flowers. Fig wasps, however, come to the rescue. They are so small that they can actually get into the plant. The male fig wasps never leave the confines of wild fig plants, but the females venture out. And when they do, they visit the Smyrna fig plants, pollinating them with pollen from wild figs. Without the female of this tiniest of species the Smyrna fig would never be able to reproduce.

THE FASTEST

On the spot
As it calls at a brightly colored plant to feed on its nectar, this tiny hummingbird hawk moth hovers on the spot so speedily that you can hardly see it move.

A small but robust hummingbird hawk moth is hovering above a flower and is about to feed on nectar through its extended proboscis. Often mistaken for the bird after which it is named, this insect has an end to its abdomen that closely resembles a hummingbird's tail. Both the bird and the moth fly with the most amazingly speedy wingbeats. Most moths are nocturnal, but this species flies by day. It is found in southern Europe, North Africa, and in parts of Asia. However, this unique moth does not only hover at a fantastic rate. Although it has a wingspan of just two inches, it can speed through the air at a breathtaking 43 miles per hour.

A close-up shows the back and wings of a dragonfly. This insect can speed along at up to 65 miles per hour over short distances.

▲▲ **Superswimmer**

The male great diving-beetle above is only around 1.5 inches long but a very speedy swimmer and a ferocious predator, as are its larvae, sometimes called water tigers because they are such swift hunters.

The rapid robberfly ▲▲

Other insects have to be wary when robberflies are around. They fly so quickly and have such lightning reactions to the presence of likely prey that there is little chance of escape.

Which insects might win an entomological Olympics, if such events existed? One species of cockroach can run a distance of 50 times its own body length in just one second! Human beings take ten times as long to run the body length of an average man. An Australian dragonfly, meanwhile, can reach a rate of 36 miles per hour – more than the speed limit for vehicles in many built-up areas. Some bees and butterflies can achieve up to 10 miles per hour. Horseflies are even swifter. Female horseflies have been seen chasing vehicles going at about 30 mph, possibly mistaking them for large animals and so a likely source of a blood-meal.

Entomologists have calculated that a hungry flea can jump 13 inches over 500 times in succession in just one hour if it is trying to find a host. If it fails in the attempt, it will repeat the exercise hour after hour until its appetite is eventually satisfied.

Tiger beetles, it is sometimes claimed, move so speedily that they are like the cheetahs of the insect kingdom. As they chase their prey, they may occasionally even take to the air and then land again to continue running. Being able to run, swim, fly, or jump fast has clear advantages and may win an insect a meal, some shelter, a mate, or escape from a predator.

THE SLOWEST

At a standstill

How different the male and female vaporer moths are! The male, on the left of the photograph above, looks and flies like a normal moth; but the female, on the right, is wingless and will stay rooted to the spot.

The immobile queen

Attended by her devoted workers, this queen termite is a giant in comparison with other termites in her colony, including the king with whom she lives and mates.

A plant stem has become infested with tiny greedy scale insects. They are serious pests; and their continual sucking at the plant's sap, if uncontrolled, could even kill the vegetation. As they feed in this way, these stationary insects are tended by ants that cannot get enough of their sweet excretion. There is no chance that these scale insects will scuttle away from them, however. Only as larvae did they move around a little. As adults, they do not budge at all.

It is hard to tell whether a few members of the insect kingdom ever move from the spot. With some sap-sucking insects, for instance, there is little need to move, since food is always on tap. Parasitic insects of all sorts are in fact usually quite happy to remain in one place for as long as a food supply lasts. Queen social insects take it easy, too, and have numerous workers to look after their every need once they start to lay. Producing up to 30,000 eggs every day, queen termites, for example, become very bloated, so it is hardly any wonder that they remain static like a giant laying machine.

AS STILL AS STATUES

Leaf insects and stick insects tend not to move much during the day, remaining skillfully camouflaged because of their coloring and shape. They will usually start moving after sunset, however, when it is safer to go looking for a meal. The pupae of insects that go through complete metamorphosis also remain still. Inside, however, during this so-called resting stage, their bodies are undergoing all sorts of amazing changes to the existing structure, and completely different-looking creatures will emerge.

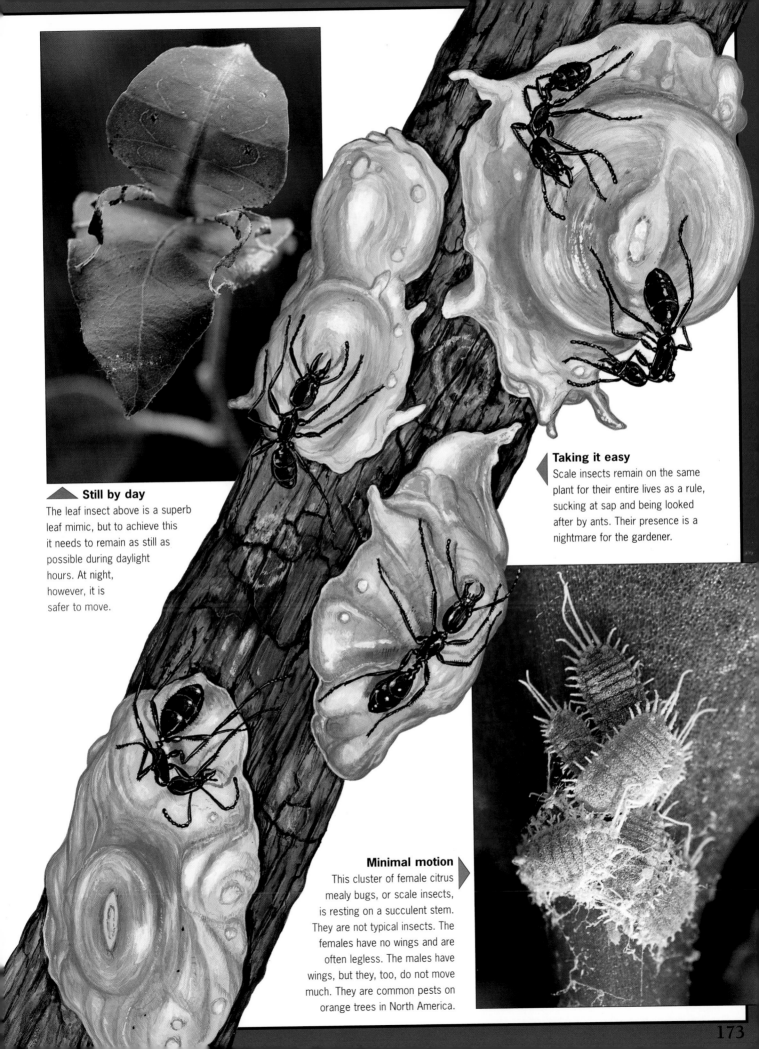

Still by day

The leaf insect above is a superb leaf mimic, but to achieve this it needs to remain as still as possible during daylight hours. At night, however, it is safer to move.

Taking it easy

Scale insects remain on the same plant for their entire lives as a rule, sucking at sap and being looked after by ants. Their presence is a nightmare for the gardener.

Minimal motion

This cluster of female citrus mealy bugs, or scale insects, is resting on a succulent stem. They are not typical insects. The females have no wings and are often legless. The males have wings, but they, too, do not move much. They are common pests on orange trees in North America.

THE RAREST

Emerging from a crack in the barren earth, a giant earwig crawls off into the night. He has been searching for days but has failed to find a mate. Suddenly, though, as he tests the edge of a crack, he picks up the scent of a female. Hurriedly, he prepares to rush in; but just as he does this, he comes face to face with a giant centipede. It has been finishing a meal of a giant female earwig. The unfortunate male earwig is too late and runs off. He may have to face the fact that, since his species is so rare, he may never reproduce.

Near extinction
Specimens of the giant earwig shown in the lower part of this illustration are jealously guarded by zoos and natural history museums since the insect is now so rarely seen in the wild. How huge the pincers at its rear are!

A rare male
The male Queen Alexandra's birdwing butterfly from Papua New Guinea is smaller than the female, shown below, but is much more spectacular in its coloring and wing patterns than she is.

A rare female
This female Queen Alexandra's birdwing is the largest known butterfly in the world and, like the male, very rare. Both are now listed as endangered species and are protected by international law.

Many animals around the world have become endangered, but few are becoming extinct as speedily as the insects. In the time that it takes you to read this book, quite a few species may have died out. It may be difficult to believe, but scientists have estimated that if mammals disappeared at the same rate as insects, there would be none left at all in a few months from now. Some species of insects have become so reduced in numbers that none has been seen for years. Others have only been spotted once before disappearing back into impenetrable forests. Why, though, do insects suddenly become extinct? Sometimes it can be due to overcollection by enthusiasts, and this is certainly how some species of butterflies have disappeared. In some countries, parts of North America included, there are strict laws now against collecting rare insects. The destruction and pollution of natural habitats is the most serious problem, however.

THE GREEDIEST

A gardener cannot believe his eyes. Yesterday afternoon his favorite shrub had been in peak condition, ready for display at a horticultural show. Yet by this morning half of the leaves appeared to have been chewed to bits. Scores of tiny caterpillars had eaten their way around the foliage. They prefer to eat at night to avoid the attention of predators. There is nothing that the gardener can do to revive his plant. The greedy caterpillars have had their fill and have ruined his chances of winning this year's champion grower award.

Crazy for sugar

In the photograph below, a male hornet is lapping up sugar solution. This large wasp likes nothing better than sweet substances, as do all wasps. This is why, if you picnic in summer and bring sweet food with you, chances are that you will be disturbed by the approach of greedy wasps. If they come near, leave them alone, or they may sting.

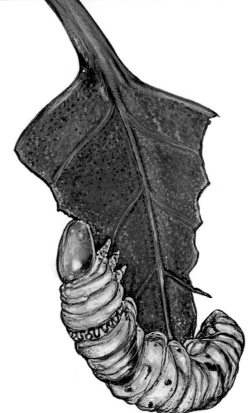

Nibbling away

Follow the sequence of illustrations from left to right and marvel at the eating capacity of a caterpillar as it munches all the way around a leaf several times its own body size.

Caterpillars eat greedily, but locusts cause far more extensive devastation to crops when swarms of them land. Insects that excel at sucking sap – thrips and aphids, for instance – are also very greedy. They even make two types of saliva. One is injected to form a sheath around their mouthparts so that sucking can go on freely through this "straw." The other breaks down the cell walls of the plant. Scorpionflies, meanwhile, are among the most successful scavengers, and wasps and bees cannot resist anything sweet.

QUALITY COUNTS

Some insects can get through their lives without eating much at all. However, for others, particularly at the growing stage, large meals are important. If the insect is very active and runs or flies a lot, it will need an almost constant supply of food to keep its muscles in good working order. But in general, the *quality* of the food eaten governs how much an insect needs to eat. If its diet is low in nutrients, the insect will have to eat vast amounts in order to grow at the larval stage and keep healthy.

Amazing appetites

In the heart of a forest in Thailand a praying mantis has been caught on camera as it starts to eat a meal of gecko. Mantises are constantly hunting and seem to have insatiable appetites.

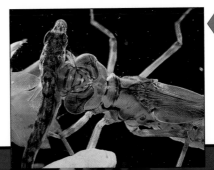

Larval feeding

This South African dragonfly larva is eating a stickleback – one more example of how much more greedy larvae often are than the adult form of an insect.

177

THE MOST DANGEROUS

Feared fly
This tsetse fly has a bloated abdomen after a human blood meal. It is a carrier of sleeping sickness.

The Kalahari bushman first had to locate the right sort of tree and then started to dig. In just a few minutes he collected a handful of little leaf beetle grubs from within the bark. Carefully, he will now squeeze one so that its body fluids spill out onto the shaft of an arrow just behind its pointed tip. His next step will be to sneak up on a large antelope that he has noticed feeding nearby. He will then aim and fire. The small arrow will make only a tiny wound in the animal's neck, but that is all that is needed. The poison on the end of the arrow is sufficiently strong to bring down the creature. The bushman and his immediate family, as well as others in the tribe, will feast tonight in the open – on antelope steaks.

Poisoned arrows
Some of the world's peoples who live close to nature are more aware of insect behavior. The bushmen of the Kalahari, for example, know only too well how poisonous some beetle grubs are and put their venom to use when shooting arrows at African game.

Allergic responses

The German wasp innocently seeking nectar on this flower will sting if annoyed, and anyone who is hypersensitive may have a terrible reaction to the venom.

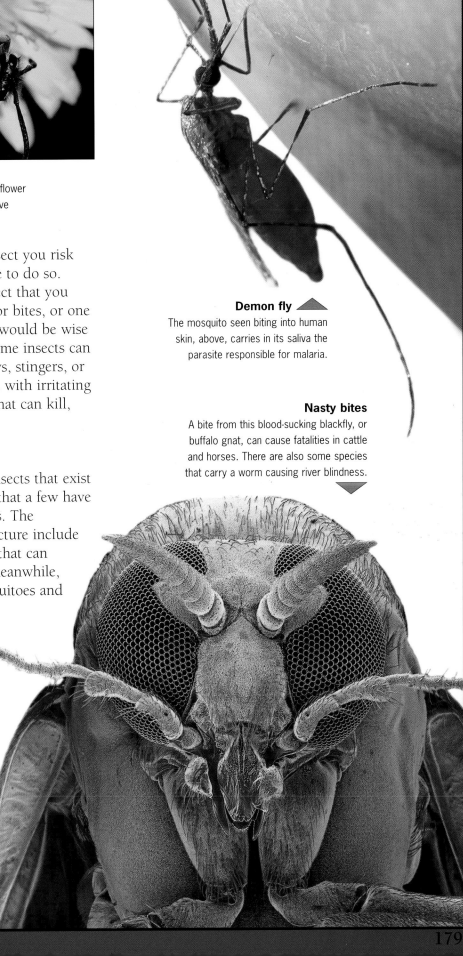

Although when you handle an insect you risk picking up germs, it is generally safe to do so. However, if you come across an insect that you know is poisonous, one that stings or bites, or one with which you are unfamiliar, you would be wise to think twice before grabbing it. Some insects can cause painful wounds with their jaws, stingers, or spines, while others may be covered with irritating hairs. There are even a few insects that can kill, including some types of bees.

HARMFUL REACTIONS

With all the millions of species of insects that exist on the earth, it is hardly surprising that a few have developed powerful defense systems. The chemicals that these insects manufacture include acids, nerve toxins, and substances that can cause intense pain. Other insects, meanwhile, may spread serious diseases – mosquitoes and tsetse flies, for instance.

Some insects, of course, are deadly to other insects. The praying mantis is a fearsome killing machine and will even eat her mate. Assassin bugs will camouflage themselves with termite feces and then kill so that they can have a termite feast. Termites are themselves, however, dangerous to some species of ants and will frequently bite them in half or explode, committing a form of hara-kiri as they spray a sticky yellow matter.

Demon fly

The mosquito seen biting into human skin, above, carries in its saliva the parasite responsible for malaria.

Nasty bites

A bite from this blood-sucking blackfly, or buffalo gnat, can cause fatalities in cattle and horses. There are also some species that carry a worm causing river blindness.

179

THE LONGEST-LIVED

Forty-five years ago a female longhorn beetle quietly laid her eggs in a piece of felled timber and then promptly abandoned them so that the larvae would have to fend for themselves. She could not have known that the very piece of wood in which she had deposited her eggs was part of a consignment to be sent across the ocean from Great Britain to the United States of America to be made into kitchen furniture. Day after day for nearly half a century, these larvae chewed away at the wood from inside the timber. Who would have thought that all those years later, several pairs of jaws would finally break through the surface of a chair!

The veteran queen
This termite queen from Malaysia will be the longest survivor in her colony. Millions of her offspring will die before she does.

Most of us think of insects as short-lived creatures, lasting only a few months at the most. The majority have certainly sacrificed a long life for a rapid turnover of generations, which gives them the best possible chance of adapting to changing conditions. However, there are some insects that still manage to survive for several years, usually as larvae. Those that have a diet that is nutritionally poor – the wood-eaters, for instance – take a very long time to reach their adult stage. Others are so tough that they may even spend several years in a type of suspended animation.

The periodic cicada only reaches adulthood after 13 or 17 summers, when they suddenly all emerge together, as if by some sort of prearranged signal. Queen ants and termites are long-lived by insect standards, too.

After 17 summers
The periodic cicada, left, is finally emerging from its last molt on a tree in New Jersey. It spent 17 years getting to this stage in an underground environment. As with all other insects that have a long developmental stage, the adult life is comparatively very short.

Out at last!

The longhorn beetles that are clambering all over the chair in this illustration spent almost 50 years as larvae in the wood from which the furniture was made before emerging as adults.

A long larval life

Although this metallic wood-boring beetle, photographed in the Amazon rainforest of Peru, does not have a long developmental period, its larval stage will still have been longer than its adult life.

Secure in its cell

Photographed in the Czech Republic, this beetle pupa is secure in a cell within an oak tree. You spend about 16 years growing and then have perhaps 64 years as an adult. With insects, as demonstrated over these two pages, it is the growth stage that is frequently far longer.

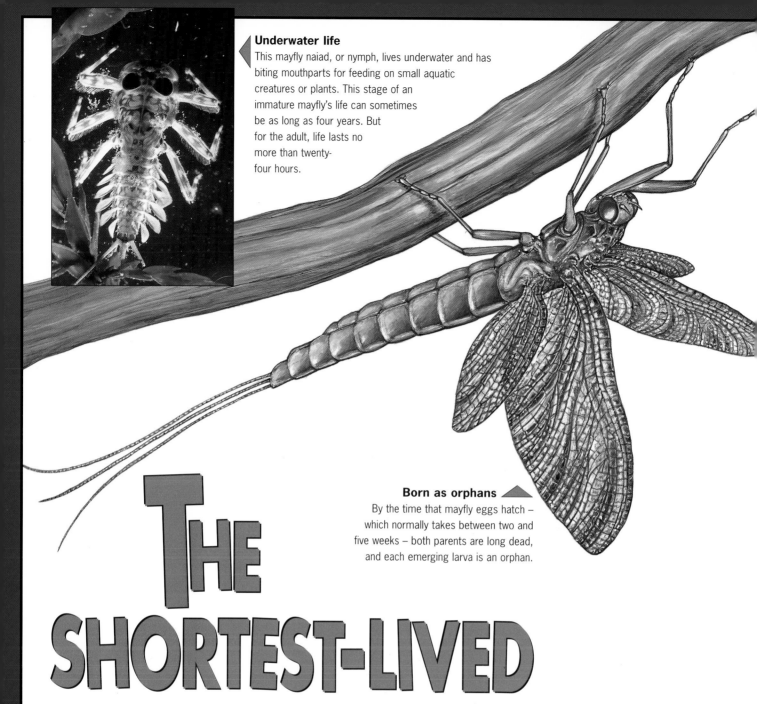

Underwater life

This mayfly naiad, or nymph, lives underwater and has biting mouthparts for feeding on small aquatic creatures or plants. This stage of an immature mayfly's life can sometimes be as long as four years. But for the adult, life lasts no more than twenty-four hours.

Born as orphans

By the time that mayfly eggs hatch – which normally takes between two and five weeks – both parents are long dead, and each emerging larva is an orphan.

THE SHORTEST-LIVED

A male mayfly is about to take to the air for the first time and has just begun his adult life. After only a few hours of flying, like others of his species, he will start to feel tired, and food reserves will be running low. Soon he joins a swarm holding vast numbers of his kind, and all begin the search for a mate. There is great competition for females, like the one in the illustration above, who enter the swarm from above, sometimes flying as high as fifty feet. After dancing up and down for a while, thanks to his enlarged eyes (far bigger in the males than in female mayflies) he does find a partner, and they get together in the air. Before long, he is too exhausted to fly any further and slowly settles on the ground. By morning he will have died of old age. The female will have returned to the water, but here her body will literally explode as she releases her minute eggs.

▲ **Flying at last**
This adult mayfly, photographed in New South Wales, Australia, waits for its wings to dry before taking to the air.

Mayflies, easily recognized by the three "tails" at their rear, are perhaps more familiar to anglers than to entomologists. They spend their egg and nymph stages underwater, where fish often eat them. That is why fly-fishermen often base the artificial flies they make on mayflies.

These insects also frequently fly into houses, especially at night, when they are attracted by lights. You might suppose, from their name, that these insects are only to be found during one month. However, they are out and about in many parts of the world throughout the summer – but only for a day or so. Indeed, the order to which mayflies belong is known as *Ephemeroptera*, meaning "winged creature living for a day." The nymph stage, however, may last up to two years.

NONFEEDERS

Sometimes a mayfly may emerge in the evening and not even last until the following morning. A few, however, live for as long as a week but cannot feed because their mouthparts are closed and their stomachs full of air.

Longer-living mayflies may sometimes keep their eggs inside their bodies until they are ready to hatch. When each nymph has matured, possibly after overwintering, it leaves the water speedily yet carefully to rest on a stone. Its skin then splits so that the adult emerges and flies away. There is one more molt to come, however.

Only for a day ▲
It is evening, and a mayfly pauses to rest by the water. It may find a mate before dawn, but within hours both will have lost their very short adult lives.

Most extraordinary is the fact that such fragile and short-lived insects should have become fossilized over millions of years, so that there is evidence of their existence in prehistoric times.

HIGHLY SENSITIVE

Today, mayflies are known to be highly sensitive to pollutants. They are therefore frequently used as bioindicators by water authorities who study the purity of watercourses. Some mayflies burrow into the underwater sediments at the nymph stage, using their jaws or their legs. This disturbance causes pollutants, such as pesticides that are not normally water soluble, to become absorbed at greater depths. Once they are at this level, they will pose less risk to fish, aquatic insects, and to the ecosystem generally.

There are well over two thousand species of mayflies. Those known commonly as coffinflies are found near sandy-bottomed lakes and rivers. The males die after mating, when their bodies can be found in piles more than two feet deep.

THE SMELLIEST

A bombardier beetle has suddenly been disturbed and reacts by scaring off a predator in a very specialized way. It does not actually attack its enemy – that would be too risky. It retaliates instead in a far more unexpected fashion and noisily releases from its rear a squirt of smokelike gas that not only smells disgusting but is hot and would burn if it came into contact with your skin. It is particularly offensive to predatory insects, as well as spiders, rodents, and birds that like to feast on beetles. The rat that threatened to make a meal of this beetle is at once put off.

A stinker
This giant female stick insect is very smelly, which helps keep predators at bay.

Smoke bombs
Bombardier beetles produce their own peculiar aroma in the form of a smoke bomb, as shown here. This is not to attract a mate, however. Instead, the boiling hot, smelly, smokelike gas is released from their rear to retaliate against an enemy.

A particularly good shot, the bombardier beetle can aim its nasty gas discharge directly at its enemy. Ants have even been seen to develop seizures as a reaction to the acrid discharge, which smells like nitric acid. No other creature is likely to come near the beetle for a while, allowing it the chance to make an escape. Even an insect as greedy as a praying mantis would be deterred by the release of such powerful chemicals and decide to leave this beetle alone.

CHEMICAL WARFARE

When the bombardier beetle launches its explosive weapon, chemicals including hydrogen peroxide are released into an area near the tip of the abdomen that opens into a combustion chamber. Enzymes are simultaneously released, and a violent, offensive chemical reaction occurs to the accompaniment of a loud popping sound. Enemies immediately retreat.

Insects use smells for several different reasons, defense being among the most common. Some stick insects, for example, will release smelly potent chemicals that they force into the air with powerful contractions of the abdomen if a zookeeper happens to pick them up, making him choke and sneeze violently. Ladybugs, though pretty to look at, will give out a yellow fluid that tastes awful, as will the aptly named stink bugs, their bright coloring and noxious perfume clearly advertising the fact that they are not to be tampered with. Some grasshoppers become equally smelly if attacked and produce a blue foam from the thorax that is very unpleasant.

Most such defensive reactions take place outdoors, of course; but if you happen to catch a whiff of something that has rotted in the kitchen, it might not be the lingering aroma of last night's supper but the calling card of cockroaches.

There are darkling beetles, too, that sometimes seem about to stand on their heads. Raising their abdomens, they then spray a jet of repellent liquid. Some lacewings – pretty little green insects with yellow eyes – will take enemies unawares and resist attack in a similar way.

▲ **True to their name**
The squash bug in this photograph does a lot of damage to squash fruits in the United States. It is also known as a stink bug because of the horrible smell of its secretions.

Odorous desert-dwellers
Desert skunk beetles, like the three shown below, will spray offensive chemicals from their abdomens if disturbed. The smell is so foul that they definitely deserve the name "skunk" – an animal that also has a reputation for giving out nasty odors.
▼

With a click

If a click beetle falls on its back, it can throw itself in the air and right itself with a distinct clicking noise.

THE NOISIEST

After 17 years of complete silence an adult male cicada prepares to sing for the first time. He has climbed up a tree so that he will be heard over a large distance. Soon the silence of the night is shattered by an ear-splitting burst of song, and everyone within a mile of the cicada will know that he is around. There are many insects that sing loudly – crickets, for example, and katydids. But the prize for the most noisy should surely be awarded to the cicada.

Tapping away

This beetle from the Namib Desert in Africa belongs to a species that has a habit of knocking on the ground to attract a mate. It will raise its abdomen and then bang it down.

On certain nights of the year in many tropical countries, the noise created by cicadas is quite deafening. They use a unique method of sound production. Instead of rubbing two parts of the body together, they call on organs known as *tymbals* on either side of the abdomen. A ring of powerful muscles holds the thin, flexible membrane of each tymbal rigid, just as the skin of a drum is held taut. As the muscles relax, the membrane makes a sound similar to that made if you wobble a piece of tin or board. When the muscles contract, the membrane becomes rigid again and repeats the sound.

Loud and clear

Male meadow grasshoppers sing by rubbing part of their hind legs over a corrugated area of each wing. The sound produced is loud and strident.

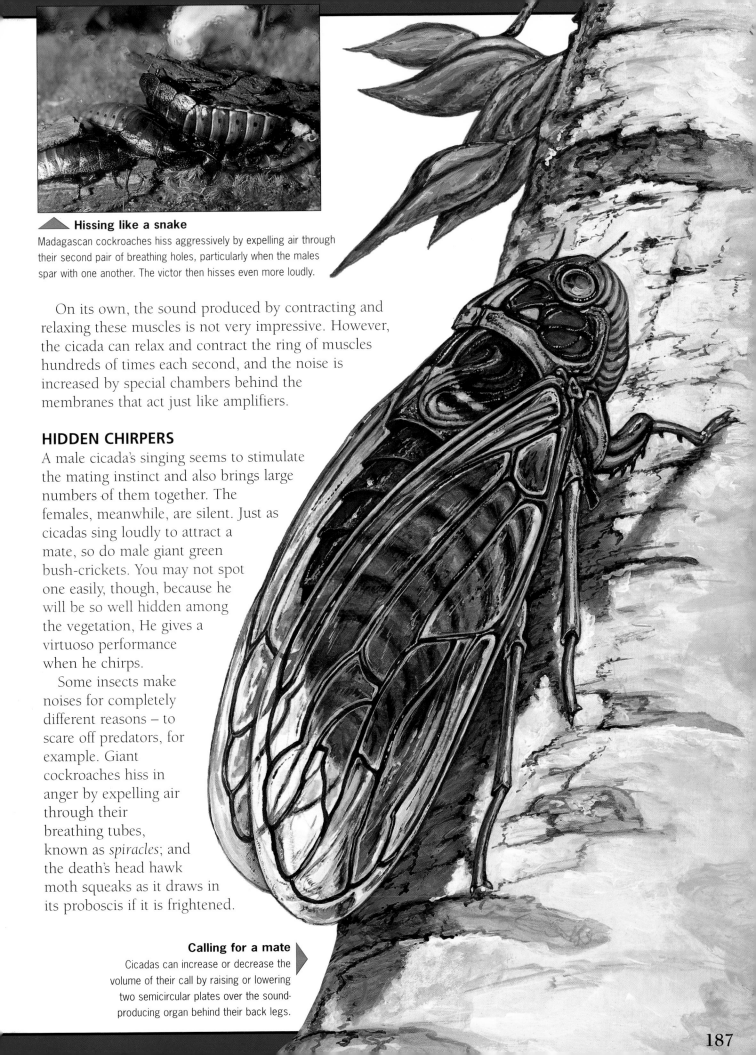

Hissing like a snake

Madagascan cockroaches hiss aggressively by expelling air through their second pair of breathing holes, particularly when the males spar with one another. The victor then hisses even more loudly.

On its own, the sound produced by contracting and relaxing these muscles is not very impressive. However, the cicada can relax and contract the ring of muscles hundreds of times each second, and the noise is increased by special chambers behind the membranes that act just like amplifiers.

HIDDEN CHIRPERS

A male cicada's singing seems to stimulate the mating instinct and also brings large numbers of them together. The females, meanwhile, are silent. Just as cicadas sing loudly to attract a mate, so do male giant green bush-crickets. You may not spot one easily, though, because he will be so well hidden among the vegetation, He gives a virtuoso performance when he chirps.

Some insects make noises for completely different reasons – to scare off predators, for example. Giant cockroaches hiss in anger by expelling air through their breathing tubes, known as *spiracles*; and the death's head hawk moth squeaks as it draws in its proboscis if it is frightened.

Calling for a mate

Cicadas can increase or decrease the volume of their call by raising or lowering two semicircular plates over the sound-producing organ behind their back legs.

GLOSSARY

ABDOMEN
Rear section of an insect's body, containing its digestive and reproductive organs

AGGREGATION
Occurs when insects huddle together to keep warm

ALATES
Winged termites

ALGAE
Primitive plants found in water, and without true stems, leaves, or roots

ALLERGIC
Having a bad reaction to a substance

ANTENNAE
Sensory organs found in pairs on the head of an insect

ANUS
The opening through which waste products are passed

ARTHROPODS
Any small creatures with jointed limbs and a hard exoskeleton. Insects are arthropods.

BATESIAN MIMICRY
A type of mimicry in which one species is protected from danger by taking on the appearance of another

BIOINDICATOR
Providing information about the state of the environment

BIOLUMINESCENCE
A light given out naturally by an insect as a signal

CAMOUFLAGE
Occurs when a creature blends in with its surroundings

CANNIBAL
A creature eating its own kind

CATERPILLAR
The larva of a moth or butterfly

CERCI
Feelers at the rear of the abdomen of some insects

CHITIN
A tough, lightweight material forming an insect's exoskeleton or outer covering

CHRYSALIS
Another name for a pupa

COCOON
A case in which an insect changes from a larva into a pupa or chrysalis

COLONY
A group of insects living together

CROP
A special stomach in which some insects store food

DECIBELS
A measurement of the loudness of sound

DRONES
Male bees

ECOSYSTEM
The interaction of all living organisms

ENTOMOLOGIST
A scientist who studies the body structure and behavior of insects

ENZYME
a substance produced by a living cell and playing a part in a chemical reaction

EXOSKELETON
An insect's outer covering

EXTINCT
No longer existing

FECES
Excrement

FILE
A ridged structure that some insects use to produce sound

FORAGER
A worker bee that goes out to look for a source of nectar for the rest of the hive

FURCULA
An organ near the rear of a springtail that is released, like a catch, so that it is tossed into the air

GALL
An unusual growth that can be found on a plant or tree, caused by the young of various insects and within which they develop

HEMOLYMPH
An insect's blood

HALTERES
An insects' balancing organs

HERMAPHRODITE
A single creature with both male and female reproductive organs

HIBERNATION
Resting throughout the cold months of the year when food is often scarce

KERATIN
A substance forming the outer layer of an insect's body covering

LARVA
A stage in the life of insects going through complete metamorphosis, occurring between the egg and pupal stages

MANDIBLES
An insect's jaws

METAMORPHOSIS
Takes place when insects change from being eggs to adults. In complete metamorphosis, insects – such as butterflies – change completely. Insects undergoing incomplete metamorphosis – such as cockroaches and dragonflies – look more like adults as they develop

MIMICRY
Copying the behavior and appearance of another creature

MITOCHONDRIA
Tiny powerhouses that help produce bioluminescence

MOULTING
Occurs when an insect loses an outer layer of skin

NIT
A head louse egg

NUPTIAL
Before mating

NYMPH
Stage between the egg and adult form in incomplete metamorphosis

OCELLI
Small extra eyes found in some insects

OOTHECA
A protective bag in which some insects carry their eggs

OPERCULUM
An opening in the eggs of some insects through which they hatch

OVIPAROUS
Describes insects laying eggs

OVIPOSITOR
A tube through which some female insects lay their eggs

OVOVIVIPAROUS
Describes insects keeping their eggs inside their bodies until they hatch

PALEOBOTANIST
A scientist who studies the fossils of plants and trees

PALEONTOLOGIST
A scientist who studies animal fossils

PARASITE
A member of a species that feeds off a member of another

PARTHENOGENETIC
Reproducing without the need for mating

PEDICEL
The waist of a wasp

PESTICIDE
A chemical that kills pests

PHEROMONES
Chemicals released by insects as sexual attractants, alarm signals, or trail-markers

POLLINATE
To fertilze a plant. The male sex cell, the pollen, is introduced to the female part of a plant, the ovule

POLLUTANT
A harmful substance that pollutes or contaminates – industrial waste, for instance

PROBOSCIS
Elongated insect mouthparts

PUPA
The stage between the larva and the adult form of insects undergoing complete metamorphosis

QUEEN
A sole egg-layer in some insect colonies, such as those of bees, wasps, ants, and termites

QUEEN SUBSTANCE
A special food produced by the queen bee

RECTUM
The last part of the gut

REPLETE
A bloated ant from which other ants feed

RESILIN
An elastic substance that helps some insects leap

ROSTRUM
An extension of the mouthparts of some insects

ROYAL JELLY
A substance rich in sugars, fed to the queen honeybee by her colony

SAP
A nutrient-rich liquid in plants

SCOUTS
Insects that go out from a nest to look for new homes or food sources

SCRAPER
A ridged surface drawn over the file when some insects stridulate

SEDUCIN
A hormone

SPIRACLES
Breathing holes

STRIDULATE
To make a sound either by rubbing two parts of the body against each other or by vibrating a special membrane

SWARMING
Occurs when insects gather in large numbers to mate, feed, or migrate to a new area

TEGMINA
Wing cases

THORAX
The central part of an insect's body, between the head and the abdomen

TROPHALLAXIS
Exchange of food between two members of an insect colony

TYMBAL
A membrane which will produce sound in some insects when stretched

VENOM
Poison emitted by some insects, causing pain, and perhaps paralysis or even death, in other creatures. Humans can have a bad reaction to venom, too

VIVIPAROUS
Producing live young

INDEX